Understanding and Loving Your Bonus Child

UNDERSTANDING AND LOVING YOUR BONUS CHILD

STEPHEN ARTERBURN
and **CONNIE CLARK, Ph.D.**

SALEM
BOOKS
an imprint of Regnery Publishing
Washington, D.C.

Salem Books™ is a trademark of Salem Communications Holding Corporation. Regnery® is a registered trademark and its colophon is a trademark of Salem Communications Holding Corporation.

Cataloging-in-Publication data on file with the Library of Congress

ISBN: 978-1-68451-156-3
eISBN: 978-1-68451-319-2

Library of Congress Control Number: 2022938959

The authors are represented by the literary agency of WordServe Literary (www.wordserveliterary.com).

Published in the United States by
Salem Books
An Imprint of Regnery Publishing
A Division of Salem Media Group
Washington, D.C.
www.SalemBooks.com

Manufactured in the United States of America

10 9 8 7 6 5 4 3 2 1

Books are available in quantity for promotional or premium use. For information on discounts and terms, please visit our website: www.SalemBooks.com.

From Connie
To my husband Ken
The greatest love of my life
The one who made me a bonus mom to
Casey, Kegan, and Erika

To my grandmother Rena
Who was the first to show me DNA doesn't make you family,
LOVE does

From Steve
To my bonus boys Carter and James
Who are two all-expectations-exceeded blessings in my life

CONTENTS

Introduction

It is not a secret that I was in a painful twenty-year marriage that ended when I confronted my previous wife about her unfaithfulness and she filed for divorce. There was no scandal, just a tragedy. I feared for my daughter, Madeline, who was eleven at the time. I knew the statistics about children of divorce, and I set out to make sure she was the exception, or at least do the best I could to that end. She lived with me, and we began our difficult journey together.

To provide some early hope here, Madeline was the exception. She didn't use drugs or alcohol or have sex in high school. She was accepted at Azusa Pacific University based on her character alone. She graduated with a degree in occupational therapy with highest honors. She is strong and self-sufficient and possesses very good judgment. When the time came, I officiated her wedding.

At that wedding, Madeline was stunningly beautiful. Everyone I spoke to was happy for her and Tim, and they could not say enough about how beautiful she looked. We danced to "Unforgettable" by Nat King Cole, as tears rolled down my cheeks. It took all I had not to break down completely from the pure joy of the moment. After a few minutes, we were interrupted: Carter wanted to cut in.

Carter is twenty-four—my bonus son and Madeline's stepbrother from the blended family Misty and I put together over seventeen years ago. But to Madeline, he is simply her brother, and he wanted to honor her by being part of the dance. They talked and laughed until their brother James, my twenty-two-year-old bonus son, cut in for an all-smiles spin across the floor. That ended when the first child Misty and I had together, Solomon, fifteen, cut in because he did not want to be left out. Finally, before I stepped back in and finished the dance, our daughter Amelia, twelve, stepped in for what she called the best part of the greatest night of her life.

Throughout the evening people continued to comment on what an amazing family we have and how obvious it is that we all love each other, like being together, and were there in every way for Madeline. I am not sharing this so I can take credit for our amazing family. It could be in spite of me and more a result of my great partner, Misty. Plus, children are not robots; they make their own choices, and we are fortunate that they chose to love, accept, and enjoy each other.

Having said that, there are some principles Misty and I followed that laid a foundation for a healthy, happy, loving blended family. I will share those principles alongside Connie Clark's great work throughout the rest of this book.

■ ■ ■

It might shock you to know that when two people, each of them with children from a previous marriage, want to marry each other, it is usually a bad idea. That isn't the result of a bad attitude or negativity—it's just what science shows us: 70 percent of blended families fail. Knowing that fact and believing it to be true, a wise person would: 1) go slowly into marriage and 2) thoroughly prepare beforehand.

This book is a thorough resource to prepare yourself for a strong and secure marriage with a blended family. Dr. Connie Clark has done the heavy lifting for this book. I wanted to work with her on this project because, first of all, she is one of the best therapists in the New Life network of Christian counselors, coaches, therapists, and psychologists. She had tremendous respect from her peers as both a brilliant educator and an extremely effective practitioner. As you will see as you read on, she has been where you and I have been. This material is from her heart and experience, not just concepts learned from a class or a textbook. Her revealing the mistakes she made (as we all have) and what she did about them is some of the most valuable material in the book. Finally, this book is not just about raising bonus children and blending families. It is about honoring God, implementing biblical truth and principles, and integrating a strong and solid faith in all aspects of marriage and parenting. Connie is theologically sound and effective in integrating faith into the bonus parenting concepts that matter most. You can be assured as you start this book that Connie's research, experience, and wisdom—along with some of my insights as a father to bonus children—will prepare you to parent kids who were not originally yours. To avoid confusion and make for easy reading, unless noted, the writing is in Dr. Clark's voice. It is a strong one that can be trusted.

But this is not a book just to help fathers and mothers prepare to take on a blended family. It is written to help you repair any struggle, conflict, or damage that has already been done. The tools are here to repair the deepest hurts.

One caveat: this material is only helpful to those who are humble and willing to search their hearts for defects, examine the impact of their behaviors on others, and willingly make changes to become a godly influence rather than an ungodly, destructive force.

That is the path to being a bonus parent who blesses all the children. It is the path that helps you see stepchildren as a blessing, not a burden. As you read on, I invite you to evaluate yourself, not the children. Ask if you are right for them—not if they have been raised right. Determine that you can be part of the 30 percent of blended families that not only make it, but make it well.

This book will show you how to earn the respect of your bonus children, rather than demand it. Seek out ways to show your love rather than wait for a child to figure out how to love you. Learn how to enter and engage in their lives and their world rather than expect them to engage with you at their convenience.

It is never easy for us to change directions, but it is easier than landing in a relationship that was never going to work and never meant to be. Please read thoughtfully.

Stephen Arterburn
March 2022

CHAPTER 1

The Bad, the Ugly, and the Good News about Bonus Families

With tears spilling down her cheeks, Stephanie, a thirty-five-year-old stepmom, sat in my counseling office sighing dejectedly. "I just can't keep going on like this! There is so much bickering and constant anger in our house." Her shoulders slumped as she continued, "I love their dad with all my heart and without a doubt know God brought us both together to have a second chance at love. But the kids are making our lives miserable. When they are with us, they walk around sulking and will not look at either of us when we talk to them. Why can't they accept things and just be happy for us?"

Being in a stepfamily is often hard. In fact, in can be extremely hard. Stepfamilies are built upon loss—either through divorce or death. They are way more complicated than first families and have very different dynamics, so first-family strategies don't always work. There are many challenges, and emotions are usually very charged and intense. Marriage in itself is hard work, and when you add a blended family to the mix along with ex-spouses, financial stress, differing beliefs on parenting, and children who are still hurting over their parents' divorce or a death, it is no wonder some people do not want to be in a stepfamily. Blended families are exhausting, complex, and messy. Combining two totally different households can be one of the most challenging things a family will ever face.

Most adults are not prepared for being in a stepfamily any more than the children are. Typically, adults in stepfamilies only have the experiences of a first family, but suddenly, they are trying to parent children who may be unfamiliar and uncomfortable with them. The stepparent role is vague and complex, and most don't really know how to find the right balance of parenting. It can be frustrating to try to have a relationship with an unrelated child with little history of interaction.

Children are usually not prepared for being in a stepfamily, either. They may secretly hope their parents will get back together after a divorce—but when one parent remarries, that hope is dashed, leading to resentment. There may be pain and trauma inside their hearts, and they silently (or vocally!) grieve. On top of their grief, children may feel guilt over divided loyalties. Some children may even try to sabotage their parent's new relationship.

As I considered which topics to cover in this book, I thought back over the thirty years I've been a psychotherapist and the struggles my stepfamily patients have shared in our counseling sessions. I thought about the many times I told divorcing parents or those looking to remarry, "Focus on the kids." I realize it's hard to focus on the children when you have found the perfect mate and your life is finally filled with happiness after sorrow. Many times, I wanted to tell couples considering remarriage with stepchildren not to do it. It's hard on everyone, especially the children. Although I do believe in second chances, I also know that second chances can be more difficult than the first relationship. They are more complicated because of the additional family members: children, extended families, ex-spouses, and the ex-spouses' new partners. They are emotional because of the hurts and wounds of a family torn apart. They are difficult because in remarriage, the couple loves each other dearly and yet they may forget that their kids may not love or even like their new partner.

There's a lot I wish I'd personally known twenty-eight years ago before I started my own stepfamily with my husband, Ken, and his three amazing children. The first thing I wish someone would have told me is how hard it was going to be. My love for their dad was so easy and romantic. Being a stepmother (or "bonus mom," as our oldest son calls me) has and will continue to be a privilege I thank God for every day. My stepchildren are *my children*. My stepchildren proved that parental love has nothing to do with genetics or biology. However, becoming a stepmother to three adorable children was the hardest thing I've ever done. The emotional roller coasters were the worst part. Not because the kids were problematic, but because they were adjusting. And guess what? So were the adults.

In addition to my counseling practice, at the time I was also an associate professor of psychology and sociology, teaching classes on marriage and family. I had all this educational knowledge, so my new stepfamily would be a piece of cake, right? Hmmm, no. I was not prepared for the adjustments all of us would have to make. Yes, we had incredible family bonding times, but there were still practical matters of combining two households, getting along with the ex-spouse, communicating with multiple sets of grandparents and extended family, and dealing with all the emotions that come with being a stepfamily. As I look back, I laugh at my early attempts to manage that load. And I have shed a few tears, knowing there were times I said and did things that hurt my stepchildren. I don't pretend to be a perfect stepmother. I have failed many times. But I have learned from my experience as a stepparent, and from researching, reading, and counseling other stepfamilies. I've learned ways to correct my mistakes and do better.

You may be that stepparent too. Thankfully, forgiveness, healing, and learning can come from those experiences.

Statistics show the negative impact second families can have on marriages. The odds are not in our favor. Here are a few statistics about stepfamilies:

- Fifty percent of first marriages and 67 percent of second marriages fail.[1]
- Approximately one-third of all weddings in America today form stepfamilies.[2]
- Approximately two-thirds of all stepfamilies fail.[3]
- Thirty percent of all stepfamilies fail within the first two years. Fifty percent fail within the first six years.[4]
- Fewer than 25 percent of couples with children from previous relationships reach out for help before they marry.[5]

Yes, the statistics look discouraging, but there is good news. When stepfamilies encounter difficult times and receive information and guidance addressing specific issues, more than 80 percent go on to become stable, loving, and healthy families, according to the Stepfamily Foundation of Alberta.[6] That is what I hope this book provides: information and guidance to families seeking it.

I will share stories of people needing guidance on how to have a successful stepfamily. When the adults step up and apply suggestions from these chapters, children will begin to feel safe and centered instead of feeling caught between the people they love.

Rather than telling you how to become a stepfamily, I want to share knowledge about how to help your children adjust to their new arrangements. If the children are adjusted, the stepfamily usually succeeds. Throughout the book I will interchangeably use the terms "stepfamily" and "blended family"; "bonus child" and "stepchild."

While preparing for this book, the word *fortitude* came to mind as a theme. The definition of fortitude, according to the *Merriam-Webster Dictionary*, is "courage in pain and adversity." *Fortitude* comes from the Latin word *fortis*, meaning "strong,"[7] and in English it is used primarily to describe strength of mind. So what does fortitude have to do with stepfamilies? Everything! Look at its synonyms:

Courage—bravery—resilience—strength of character— strength of mind—toughness of spirit—firmness of purpose—forbearance—perseverance—determination

If you ask anyone who has been involved with a stepfamily, they would wholeheartedly agree with this definition and synonyms. There will be times of hardship, pain, and definitely adversity. Steve Arterburn wrote in one of his New Life daily devotionals,

> The fact that we encounter adversity is not nearly as important as the way we choose to deal with it. When tough times arrive, we have a clear choice: we can begin the difficult work of tackling our troubles...or not. When we summon the courage to look our problems squarely in the eye, [they] usually blink. But, if we refuse to address our problems, even the smallest annoyances have a way of growing into king-sized catastrophes.[8]

Exodus 17 tells the story of Moses standing on top of a hill watching a battle taking place between the Israelites and Amalekites on the plain below, holding his arms in the air. As long as they are raised, the Israelites are winning. However, the battle goes on for a long time and his arms get tired. Whenever he lowers them, the Amalekites start winning. Finally, Moses cannot hold his arms up any longer, so his brother, Aaron, and a friend named Hur each hold one of his hands in the air until the Israelites win the battle.

Think of your stepchildren as Moses: they have gone through a family divorce or a death, and are now trying to adjust to a new family. Think of yourselves, the parents, as Aaron and Hur, standing alongside your children, helping them succeed. Walk beside your stepchildren and support them as they deal with the difficulties in their new lives. They really are in a battle, and they are exhausted.

Fundamentally, *Understanding and Loving Your Bonus Child* is about helping stepchildren. It explores the concept of understanding your bonus child and the challenges a blended family may face, and offers strategies for meeting those challenges in order to help all of you move forward together. Challenges can include:

Accepting realities of being a stepfamily: Unrealistic expectations are common in stepfamilies and must be replaced with realities. If the unrealistic expectations are not challenged, they can become stumbling blocks on the stepfamily journey.

Understanding your stepchild's personality: Each stepfamily has members with different personalities. It's important to learn about your stepchildren's personalities as well as your own in order to adjust more smoothly.

Helping stepchildren manage stress: Children experience stepfamily stresses differently than their parents do. Parents can help children deal with stress by taking things slowly, having realistic expectations, having consistent family routines, and having one-on-one time with their biological children.

Surviving when difficulties arise: There are many difficulties in stepfamilies that can cause intense emotions in all the adults involved in the children's lives. Moms, dads, stepmoms, and stepdads have to learn to control their emotions because those responses can impact everyone. It's important to accept the reality that exes will always be part of the family. The children's well-being is determined primarily by the level of conflict between the coparents and how all the parents deal with their own intense feelings.

Communicating with your stepchild: Good communication skills are vital for keeping stepfamilies strong. When comparing stepfamilies that thrive with those that struggle, those with healthy communication skills are the ones that succeed.[9]

Strengthening your relationship with your spouse: Many new couples can become disillusioned and discouraged when the difficulties of being in a blended family arise. Things that can help are setting realistic expectations, having a foundation of trust, implementing positive daily habits in the marriage, adopting healthy ways of coping with stress, communicating effectively, having fun with your partner, and reaching out for counseling or a support group.

Applying the voice of truth: Stepfamily members must look at what they are telling themselves (self-talk) when difficulties pop up. The "voice of truth" technique includes being aware of your self-talk, removing the thoughts that are lies, and replacing the lies with the truth.

Increasing happiness in your stepchild: Happiness is a skill that can be learned, and parents can help teach their children to have a happy childhood in spite of their circumstances. These skills can include gratitude, kindness, self-discipline, understanding emotions, happiness habits, optimism, faith, confidence, and connection to others.

Increasing interpersonal skills for the whole family: Research shows that successful stepfamilies use more effective interpersonal tools than struggling stepfamilies.[10] Strong interpersonal skills are an asset that can help navigate challenges, adjustments, and day-to-day tasks.

This book emphasizes that strong stepfamilies face the same challenges that struggling stepfamilies do. However, it's how stepfamilies meet those challenges that will determine their success. Keep building into your stepchildren's lives, even if they don't respond. Be flexible so you can adjust to your stepfamily's needs.

Am I saying you need to do all the things mentioned in each chapter to have a happy stepfamily? No, but I am saying that implementing even one idea you discover can strengthen your relationship with your stepchildren. No parent is perfect; we all are learning and need encouragement.

The purpose of this book is to provide information on issues that are specific to stepfamilies, and to show that stepfamilies can flourish.

Here are six suggestions to ensure success in your stepfamily as you read this book:

1. Recognize the areas in which your stepfamily needs to change.
2. Be purposeful in identifying the actions you need to take.
3. Follow through on your commitment to act.
4. Strive for small changes, not perfection.
5. Be patient with the process. Take living as a stepfamily one day at a time.
6. Seek God's help daily, as well as the support of others.

Finally, thank you for allowing us to speak into your stepfamily. No matter your circumstances, we want to offer you a strong word of encouragement. By simply picking up this book, we know you have a desire for your stepfamily to be the best it can be. And by taking any kind of new action, you are telling yourself that change is possible—even if you are skeptical. We believe you are a person with great fortitude. Making changes takes courage as you commit to looking honestly at yourself and your stepfamily. God has selected you for your blended family in a role only you can fill. To those readers who turn the page and apply the suggestions from the chapters, we pray God will begin to work great things in your stepfamily.

CHAPTER 2

Stepfamily Truths

Here are some statements I've heard in my counseling practice over the years: "If my parents had not divorced, my life would be so much better." "It's all my stepchildren's fault." "It's my ex, she makes my life so miserable. It's her fault I feel this way." And to be honest, as a stepmother, I've said things like this as well. If we're facing challenging circumstances, it's easy to blame our misery on someone or something else.

The truth of the matter is that stepfamily life is hard. There are definitely challenges and times of feeling overwhelmed. However, everyone, whether they are in a stepfamily or not, has circumstances that are not pleasant or perfect. And when I write this, I'm not trying to be insensitive to the pain and frustration that is real in stepfamilies; I live it, so I know. But we must look at what we are telling ourselves in the midst of our circumstances.

This chapter is short but powerful. It focuses on what we tell ourselves in our thoughts. We must ask ourselves if these thoughts are truths or lies; if they are lies, we must remove them and replace them with the truth.

This technique of replacing lies with truth has been around for hundreds of years with different names. Some of my favorite psychiatrists and psychotherapists have called this technique cognitive behavioral therapy, truth therapy, or catching your thoughts. This isn't a new concept. The Bible tells us in 2 Corinthians 10:5 to "take every thought captive and make it obedient to Christ" (ESV). I have my own name for the technique: the voice of truth.

Casting Crowns, a contemporary Christian rock band, released a song in 2003 by that title.[1] When I first heard it, I thought, *This is what I've been telling my patients over the years—to listen to the voice of truth instead of the lies in their thoughts.* So when I'm helping patients challenge and replace the thoughts that are lying to them and making them miserable, I ask them, "What is the voice of truth for that lie?"

This technique is simple, fast, and effective. It doesn't take years of digging into your childhood to apply it. It's not complicated or hard to understand. Both adults and children can

learn to apply this to their thoughts and improve their relationships. It involves three easy steps:

1. Recognize your self-talk (thoughts you say to
   yourself).
2. If the self-talk is negative or full of lies, then
   remove those thoughts.
3. Immediately replace the lie or negative thought
   with the truth.

Over my years of working with stepfamilies, and living
in one with my husband and three stepchildren, I have
noticed that most of us think events and situations cause our
ups and downs, our frustrations and irritations. What we
don't realize is that our feelings and behaviors are caused
by what we tell ourselves and how we interpret the event or
situation. We interpret events through our thoughts and
beliefs.

Here are examples of replacing lies with the truth in the
areas of negative self-talk, anxiety, anger, and relationships
with others.

Negative Self-Talk

Lie: "My life is horrible. My parents hate me, or else they
would not have divorced."

Truth: "Yes, my parents are divorced, but that does not mean they hate me. They love me and show me their love in many ways. My life is complicated because of my parents' divorce, but I can still be happy and enjoy my life."

Lie: "I will never be good enough for my stepchildren. They hate my cooking and complain at every meal."

Truth: "My value as a person is not impacted by someone criticizing my cooking. I can listen to them and learn what they like and don't like to eat. I can come up with win-win solutions like teaching them to make a sandwich if they don't like what I've fixed. I choose if I will be upset or not."

Anxiety

Lie: "After my parents divorced, we moved and now I'll never have friends like I did at my old school."

Truth: "Being the new kid in school is hard and lonely at the beginning. I will look around and see if there is someone else who is sitting alone and needs a friend."

Lie: "I must get the approval of my husband's ex. After all, I have her children on the weekends, and it's important that she likes and accepts me."

Truth: "While it would be great if my husband's ex thinks well of me, I can still live perfectly well if I don't have her approval or acceptance. It's unrealistic to believe everyone is going to like me."

Anger

Lie: "It's my stepchildren's fault that I get angry. It's disgraceful when they don't do what I tell them to do."

Truth: "I am the only one who can make myself angry. It's unpleasant when my stepchildren don't do what I ask, but it's not horrible."

Lie: "I can't stand it when my ex is angry with me and she doesn't tell me why. It ruins the whole weekend when I get the kids."

Truth: "It's unpleasant when my ex is angry with me, but it's not the end of the world. I can choose to enjoy the weekend with my kids whether someone is mad at me or not."

Relationships with Others

Lie: "If my spouse would just stand up to her ex, things would be better."

Truth: "Whether my spouse stands up to her ex or not, I can choose to be happy. If my spouse chooses to stand up to her ex, this does not guarantee that things will be better. Life is full of unpleasant circumstances."

Lie: "My future is hopeless. I thought I could handle being a stepmother, but the kids hate me and I'm always fighting with my husband. I must have made a huge mistake."

Truth: "My future is not hopeless. Being a stepmother is hard for many women, not just me. And I can still be happy if my stepchildren never like me. I can still love them and treat them with respect. I can discuss concerns with my husband without us getting into a fight every time."

This technique of being aware of your self-talk, recognizing the lies, and replacing those lies with the truth needs to be an intentional daily habit. Stepfamilies can become happier by learning how to practice the techniques in this chapter. They can bring real change to each individual and to the family as a whole.

Closing Thoughts from Steve

The late Dr. Dave Stoop was my best friend for forty years. His book *Self Talk* has helped millions live a better life. The voice inside your head must not be allowed to tear you down and destroy your peace or self-confidence. Don't allow Satan to use your wonderful mind against you. Fill your thoughts with God's truth. Spend time focusing on God and just being with Him. And when your thoughts become so tyrannical that they are ripping you apart, seek out the help your inner voice is telling you is not needed. Free your mind from a past that cannot be changed or a future that cannot be controlled or predicted. Jesus left us with a comforter: the Holy Spirit. Receive that comfort and find the peace for your mind that comes from surrendering to Christ and His ways rather than allowing your mind to wander in a world of negative, false, and destructive thinking.

Key Points to Remember

- Everyone, whether they are in a stepfamily or not, has circumstances that are not pleasant or perfect.
- Stepfamily members must look at what they are telling themselves in the midst of negative situations.
- We interpret events through the lens of our thoughts and beliefs. Our feelings and behaviors are caused by what we tell ourselves about those interpretations.

CHAPTER 3

Accepting the Realities of Being a Stepfamily

Tom put his arm around his wife, Rebecca, as they sat close on my counseling sofa. Her eyes filled with tears, and she blew out a series of short breaths to gain control. "Even though I love being married to Tom and adore his son, I could never have imagined or understood the many things involved in blending two homes," she said. "I thought we would be this happy little family, but I constantly feel rejected by his son. And Tom thinks I favor my own daughter over his son." Laying her hand on Tom's knee, she added, "There are days I want to give up, but we both are committed to making this work."

In any blended family, there will be prevailing and unrealistic expectations of what a family should be. This can cause stress and strain in the new marriage. When these unrealistic expectations cannot be met, both the stepparent and the biological parent may feel frustrated and think they have failed in their roles.

Unrealistic expectations like Rebecca's of a "happy little family" are common in stepfamilies and impact all those involved, especially the children. If unrealistic expectations are not challenged and replaced with realities, they can become stumbling blocks on the journey. As I counsel stepfamilies, we discuss expectations that may be idealized, stereotypical, or naïve, and then we replace those expectations with realities. By accepting the realities of being a stepfamily, members can work towards a more peaceful coexistence. Here are some key facts to embrace:

Stepfamilies Are Different from Biological Families

There are several important realities that many of my stepparent clients said they wish they had known and accepted before they began their blended families. The first is that stepfamilies are not the same as biological families. Often, unrealistic expectations exist because stepfamilies compare themselves to biological families. The truth of the matter is that stepfamilies are very different from biological families.

The following is a partial list of differences provided by the Stepfamily Foundation:[1]

Biological Family	Stepfamily or Blended Family
There is time to form norms and structure, even before children are part of the picture	Little/no time to form norms and structure; children are already part of the picture
Positions in the family are generally known and understood	Positions in family can be misunderstood and hold tremendous potential for conflict
Few ugly myths or fairytales surrounding parenthood	Negative portrayals abound, such as "the wicked stepmother" or "abusive stepfather"
Children are bonded to both parents and want to please both	Children are torn; don't know how to act or whom to please
	Children mourn the loss of their original family and may be more vulnerable to negative influences

During our counseling sessions, I heard Rebecca often speak of "culture shock," almost as if she and Tom were making a family from two different cultures with their own distinct languages. Children entering a new stepfamily are definitely entering a new family culture, filled with new sights, new smells, and yes, new expectations. This "culture shock" can feel like being in a strange or unfamiliar place. A certain behavior may have been accepted when the child lived with just Mom or Dad, but it may not be allowed in the new step-family. Tom's nine-year-old son shared one example: "When Dad came home from work, my dog and I played roughhouse with him, rolling around on the floor and being silly. After he married my stepmom, no roughhousing was allowed in the house. I miss those times playing with my dad."

Not only do the stepfamilies themselves have unrealistic expectations, but society in general has a tendency to evaluate stepfamilies using norms that apply to biological families (or our idealized impressions of them). Because of this, stepfamilies still suffer from negative perceptions and stereotypes. For example, consider the fairy tales "Cinderella" and "Snow White," in which stepmothers are portrayed as heartless and cruel. Images of stepfathers as abusive or mean to their stepchildren also exist. These negative stereotypes need to be challenged if we really want to support stepparents in their difficult new roles.

Society—and stepparents themselves—need to accept that things are not going to be perfect in a blended family. It's just not going to happen. Rebecca gradually began to accept that the house would be full of noise, and hurtful things would be said once in a while. It's unrealistic to expect anything different. It is realistic to expect that everyone is trying the best they can to get along and work through the adjustments of becoming a stepfamily. The sooner stepparents and biological parents embrace the fact that stepfamilies are not like biological families, the quicker this can happen.

Slow and Steady Wins the Race

Another important reality that stepfamilies must embrace is the idea that slower is better. Things need to go slowly for the children—usually more slowly than the adults need or want them to. The fact that stepparents are eager to start their new lives doesn't mean kids are ready. Establishing a "one step at a time" rule will benefit everyone in the long run, especially the children.

Rebecca's desire to be a "happy little family" immediately was unrealistic, and these expectations were causing her a tremendous amount of disappointment and frustration. Many stepparents wish for an immediate sense of togetherness, but this is usually not the children's reality. Building stepparent-stepchild relationships and coming to a sense of "family" takes time—lots of it. Think years, not months. In counseling with Rebecca and Tom, we worked on a family goal of being civil to each other, rather than loving. This is a realistic expectation for new stepfamilies.

When stepfamilies blend, there are new roles for every member of the household. There are many possible relationships that can cause problems and need a lot of time to adjust to, especially at the beginning. It takes time for emotional bonds to form; sometimes this never occurs. Most children under three adapt with relative ease. Children over age five may have more difficulty. Some children are initially excited at having a "new" mother or father but later find that words like "I hate you" or "you can't tell me what to do" are potent weapons. This type of language frequently coincides with puberty. Stepparents need to remember that a thick skin is a must during these hurtful times. Although teenagers usually are the most challenging, children at any age can cause pain.

As I worked with Tom and Rebecca, I encouraged them both to try not to take things personally if their stepchildren were standoffish or hesitant about forming a relationship with them. Stepparents must remember that children are still grieving, especially at the beginning. One of the first and hardest changes for them is not being able to live with their biological parents in the same house. Instead, they are forced to live with just one parent and a new stepparent they may not be happy about or even like. Sometimes they will take their unhappiness out on the stepparent. Giving them some space and communicating acceptance, respect, and love will go a long way.

Often children of divorce blame and punish their stepparents because they see them as an obstacle to their birth parents getting back together. A fifty-two-year-old client once confessed to me that she still fantasized about her parents getting back together, regardless of the fact that both of her parents had been happily remarried for more than twenty years.

Be patient and accept that it takes time to develop a real relationship with your stepchildren. At the beginning, both the child and stepparent may feel anxious, and the relationship may seem forced or fake. Stepchildren will often put up a lot of resistance at first. Don't try to rush the relationship or believe you have to "catch up" with the biological parents. As a stepparent, you may give a lot of your time and love to your stepchildren and yet not feel as if they are returning or acknowledging it. Be patient and give them time and space. Adjustments will be easier if stepparents come into the new family with few expectations about how and when the relationships will develop. In the end, it's best if stepparents can relax, step back, and enjoy when the relationship does blossom instead of being frustrated and disappointed that it's not happening on their timetable.

Conflicting Emotions

For many stepchildren, suddenly belonging to a different family can be traumatic and heartbreaking. As they learn to adjust to new family members, emotions like rage, anger, guilt, resentment, and stress bring new confusion for children and parents alike. As a family, it's important to take everyone's needs into account and then find meaningful compromises so children can adjust to their new reality. Tom and Rebecca's kids both said they enjoyed their stepparents, but it caused them feelings of guilt. Sometimes kids have divided loyalties with their biological parents, and sometimes their guilt stems from not liking the new stepparent. Then, to compensate for those guilty feelings, they ignore or reject their stepparent. (It's no wonder Rebecca struggled with feelings of rejection!) It's important for stepparents to realize these feelings will exist as stepchildren try to work through their complicated feelings of grief and loss.

Parents can help both their stepchildren and their biological children by inviting the kids to share their feelings about their new stepparent and their new family, either alone or in a big family meeting. By simply listening and empathizing, parents will help their children accept their new situation and deal with their emotions in healthy ways.

Stepparents have their own emotions that emerge as they settle into their new families. Time and again, I hear stepparents share their sadness and frustration about others not recognizing them as a parent. Sometimes extended family may not acknowledge stepchildren, seeing them only as the new spouse's children. During a counseling session, Rebecca said, "When Tom and I married, I saw his children as my own. However, my mother didn't see it that way. When I asked why she didn't acknowledge my stepchildren's birthdays, she replied they were not really my kids and she wasn't going to pretend they were my children."

As a stepparent, you might see yourself as a parent, but that doesn't mean everyone else in your life will see it that way. It can be frustrating to have the responsibility of being a parent to your stepchildren and yet receiving no recognition for it. This can even include your stepchildren, who may not see you as a part of their family.

When working with discouraged stepparents who feel invisible or unappreciated, I remind them that their spouse sees their hard work and devotion to their kids. Someday when the kids are grown and start their own families, hopefully they will look back and appreciate the love and devotion they received. There were plenty of times like this when my own stepchildren were young. I knew only God and my husband saw the effort I was pouring into them. The children did not see it then, but now they are parents themselves and see the sacrifices all their parents—biological as well as bonus—put into raising them.

New Family Dynamics

At the beginning of a new marriage, each spouse's bond with his or her own children is most likely stronger than their bond as a couple, because parents and children have a biological bond that's been there since birth. It's realistic to embrace this fact and avoid getting in the way of this bond.

At the beginning of the new stepfamily, children are still grieving the loss of their previous family. During this time, they also grieve the loss of their parent's time and attention because the parent is focused on their new spouse. Some couples think that at the beginning of a remarriage, children need more time with the stepparent so they will become bonded, but research actually says the opposite. At the beginning of the remarriage, biological parent-child relationships are strained by the dynamic just described, and because of this vulnerability, children need more one-on-one time with their parents. When children feel more secure about their parent's love and secure in that relationship, they will be more open to a relationship with the stepparent.[2]

Witnessing the strong bond between parent and child can make the stepparent feel like an outsider at times. Have confidence that this relationship does not undermine your adult relationship. Since this was happening with Tom and Rebecca, I encouraged them to have solo time with their own biological children. This can be a routine or small moments throughout the day. The key takeaway is to realize that one-on-one time for each relationship within the stepfamily is important and needs to be maintained in order for each member to feel loved, needed, and bonded. If a stepparent does not understand this, problems can arise in both the new family and the marriage. A jealous attitude towards your stepchild will negatively affect your marriage. If you pressure your new spouse to always put you first, or you view your stepchild's needs as a threat to your marriage, you may begin to undermine all you hold dear.

Embrace the idea that even though you are a family now, there will be times when children will want quality time with only their parent, and parents will want solo time with their kids. Solo time with their parent reminds kids that they are still just as loved and cherished as before. That parent-child bond must be respected and nurtured. If by chance you are left out of an activity or event due to one-on-one time, remember: it doesn't mean they don't want you around. Go ahead and give your bonus kids and their parent room to breathe, and everyone will benefit from it.

It's not often discussed, but the reality is that stepparents *will* treat their stepchildren differently than their biological children. For example, Tom noticed Rebecca favoring her daughter over his son by letting her off easy when she didn't do her assigned chore. But when his son didn't do a chore, he received consequences. It sounds harsh that stepparents would treat their stepchildren differently, but it is reality. And stepchildren will treat their stepparents differently than their biological parents as well. For example, stepchildren will sometimes be disrespectful, saying things like, "You're not my mom; I don't have to do what you say!"

Stepchildren and stepparents will experience each other in different ways than biological parents and children, but this does not mean the stepfamily is unimportant. All families provide a source of identity and social support long after the children have grown and left the home.[3]

The Elephant in the Room

A simple fact of remarriage after divorce is that your partner's ex will likely become a major part of your life. During one of our counseling sessions, Tom jokingly said that when he married Rebecca, he essentially married her ex too. Obviously, you may not like the ex and the ex may not like you. And your spouse may not like their ex, either. However, we all have to put those feelings aside and parent the children together.

When dealing with your partner's ex, communication is key. It's important to communicate directly and not put the kids in the middle or use them as messengers. If you disagree with something your stepchild's other parent does, express your concerns in private with your partner—who has a relationship with his or her former spouse. Don't have that conversation in front of the child. Then let your partner bring it up with the ex-spouse if necessary. The idea of "picking your battles" is a good one to embrace when bringing up issues with the ex-spouse.

The ex may not live in your house, but you will feel his or her influence through your stepchildren. Children will often be blindly loyal to their biological parents and feel guilty or disloyal if they enjoy the stepparent. Be patient and encourage both biological parents to affirm to the kids that it's okay to like or even love you. It's helpful and puts everyone at ease when you include the ex-spouse in this conversation so he or she will understand you are not trying to replace them.

Often, children will live in both households, so the ex's house rules (or lack thereof) become a factor in your life. Once communication is established, both households need to be consistent with expectations, behaviors, discipline, and consequences. This unified front reduces confusion in the children, especially when they are young, and diminishes the possibility of children playing parents against each other.

Being a new stepparent can be frustrating and hard. It's a completely different experience than raising a child from birth. Yes, being a stepparent is often a thankless job, but it has its rewards. Keep reading to discover more tools to help you on this journey.

Closing Thoughts from Steve

If every couple considering blending two families would simply read what Connie has presented in this first chapter, the number of blended families that succeed would increase greatly.

There is nothing more important than to enter into the worlds of the children and see all that is ahead from their perspective. What feels so good and seems so right to you just may feel more like a hostile takeover or a hostage situation to them. Consideration for those children who are not under the spell of romance starts in the very beginning, with the first date. Please, for the sake of all humanity, do not meet the children on your first date! And don't meet them on the second date, either. Meet someplace where the kids are not. Only when you feel like the two of you might have a future would it be appropriate to meet the kids. They have had enough pain already, so different people walking in and out of their lives must not happen.

When it comes to remarriage, in addition to being sure you are free to remarry, you must consider what kind of father or mother this person would be at least as much as you consider what kind of husband or wife they might make. If you hear something like: "I demand respect, and your kids better learn to respect me," you have three options. One is to realize this is the tip of the iceberg, and you have been ignoring some other ice cubes that have been floating around. People don't magically get better when they marry; they get worse. The second option is to request that in addition to pre-marriage counseling—which you must have at all costs—you both need some pre-parenting counseling (especially the one demanding respect). The third option is to walk away from that relationship—immediately.

When Misty and I decided to marry, I had already developed a loving relationship with her boys. I was like a benevolent uncle or a Sunday School teacher. I did not expect their respect or demand it. Instead, I set out to earn it by forming a bond of trust with them. So we had fun together, I helped them do things they wanted to learn, and I took them on adventures. Any disciplining in the beginning needs to be done by the birth parent. Misty disciplined Carter and James, and I supported her in it. Meanwhile, I disciplined Madeline as Misty supported me.

I told Carter and James that some people call someone like me a "stepdad," but I wanted to be something different. I explained that I knew they had a dad and he loved them very much. I did not want to replace him and was not going to make him look bad. I wanted to be a "bonus" to the dad they already had. Having me as a bonus dad meant they would always have their dad, *plus* someone who wanted the best for them and who also would be there for them. Seventeen years later they still call me *their bonus dad*. These early choices led to the kids liking each other and then loving each other so much that they all wanted to be with each other.

When Madeline was finishing up her graduate work in occupational therapy in California, she needed to complete an internship. Rather than intern there, she applied for and obtained an internship about twenty miles from our house in Carmel, Indiana. She wanted to be with everyone one last time before marriage, so she lived with us for three months. Rather than distance herself from the rest of us, Madeline blended back in when given the chance. That is why at her wedding, her three brothers and sister did everything they could do to honor her and show their love.

Every situation is different, but this is what worked for us. What I know does not work is an angry, belligerent future spouse that you think will be nicer once you are married. If that is what you are thinking, best think about not getting married at all.

Key Points to Remember

- Stepfamilies are very different from biological families.
- Unrealistic expectations are common in stepfamilies. If unrealistic expectations are not challenged and replaced with realities, they can become stumbling blocks on your stepfamily's journey.
- Negative perceptions and stereotypes of stepfamilies need to be addressed in order for stepfamilies to succeed in our society.
- Stepchildren need a lot of time to adjust, especially at the beginning. Relationships in stepfamilies take time to develop and will not happen overnight.
- There will be confusing emotions for the stepchildren and stepparents as they adjust to each other.

- One-on-one time between the biological parent and child will help children adjust more quickly to the new stepparent and stepfamily.
- When remarriage happens after divorce, ex-spouses will be a major part of the stepfamily's life.
- Communication is the key when dealing with a partner's ex.

CHAPTER 4

The Successful Stepfamily Marriage

Quinten and Sara walked into my counseling office looking discouraged. Quinten's shoulders were slumped forward, and Sara's face was puffy and red from crying. Quinten began. "Sara and I were so in love when we first got married two years ago."

Sara added, "We both had been married before and thought we had found our true love and could have a happy family with all of our kids."

"But it hasn't worked out like we had planned," Quinten said. "It seems like all we ever do is fight over the kids, our exes, and how we parent."

"We do love each other," Sara hastened to add. "But we never have fun anymore and stress is killing our relationship. We either are picking at each other or avoiding each other."

Just like Quinten and Sara, many stepfamily couples can become disillusioned and discouraged when the difficulties of being a blended family snuff out their dreams of happiness. Stepfamily couples can be in love with each other and excited to start their new life but forget that blended families are not about what existed before—they are about a new kind of family life.

While couples are eager to have a second chance at happiness, the statistics of second marriages show a different picture. According to the U.S. Census Bureau, approximately 750,000 weddings take place each year in which one or both people have been married before—and most of those marriages end up failing. The census shows that U.S. remarriages have a divorce rate of 60 percent, whereas first marriages have a divorce rate of 50 percent. In addition, second marriages last a shorter amount of time—14.5 years compared to 20.8 years in first marriages.[1]

However, as discouraging as those statistics sound, you can take steps to make it more likely that your stepfamily marriage will succeed, which in turn will help your new blended family's happiness. This chapter will discuss key qualities of a successful remarriage.

Realistic Expectations

Beginning a new life in a second marriage is more satisfying if the couple has realistic expectations. According to a study about remarriage beliefs and how they can predict marital satisfaction, couples who adopt realistic expectations about the kind of stresses that will be part of the remarriage and stepfamily show more marital satisfaction than those who do not.[2]

Here are some of the key things you can expect to do if you want to succeed.

Be patient and take things slowly

As we mentioned previously, even though the remarried adults are excited to start their new happy life with their blended family, the children are not always as thrilled and need plenty of time to adjust. Give everyone time to adjust to the new family. It will take several years before everyone will feel like a family. And even then, your new family is just that: a new kind of constructed family with its own identity. It's unrealistic to think that because you and your new spouse are happy, the rest of your blended family will be as well.

Love is not instant

Because you and your new spouse love each other, it's easy to assume your children will love your new spouse just as much. This is not true. There is no such thing as instant love between a stepparent and stepchild. Most children instinctively love and trust their own parents, whereas they may feel the stepparent must earn their love and trust over time. The relationship can feel unnatural to the stepchildren, so it's best not to force it. And stepparents may not instantly love their stepchildren. Be patient and help the bonding process by having traditions, such as going to everyone's favorite camping or fishing spot once a month or having a favorite family outing.

Stepparents may feel rejected

Feelings of insecurity or jealousy will show up, so be ready for them. If you don't address these feelings, it will cause problems in your new marriage and in your relationships with your stepchildren. If your stepchild doesn't like you, this doesn't mean you have failed; it just means it will take time. A healthy goal would be for both of you to build your relationship upon respect until you get to know each other better.

Foundation of Trust and Intimacy

A successful remarriage requires a foundation of trust and intimacy. Creating and maintaining this foundation is an ongoing process that will help you deal with the challenges that will show up in stepfamily life. Here are some ways to build trust and intimacy in your marital relationship.

Be trustworthy

Being there for your partner builds trust. Show your partner that he or she is your number one priority by doing what you say you are going to do, being on time, and putting away the cell phone and looking directly at them when they are talking to you. Life can keep us busy, so show your partner how important he or she is to you.

Tune in to your partner

Relationships are about being there for your partner when they need you. If your partner is hurting or needs your support, stop what you are doing and engage with them. When we are attuned to our partner, we turn to them and help calm and soothe them when they are hurting or disappointed. Eliminate distractions by silencing your phone, turning off the television, or going to a quiet place so you can give them your undivided attention. Sometimes your partner may want to share with you about their day. It may not be about a problem; they may just want to discuss something that happened. We all want to be seen and understood when we are hurting or need to share a moment. Be careful not to minimize your partner's concerns as he or she is sharing; your spouse needs to know that sharing with you is safe, and that you are supportive. If you find yourself too busy and having a hard time finding moments to be attuned to your partner, it may be time to look at your schedule and let go of some things in order to free up some time to have one-on-one moments with him or her.

Fondness and Admiration

According to John Gottman, a professor of psychology at the University of Washington and director of the Relationship Research Institute, fondness and admiration are "two of the most crucial elements in a rewarding and long-lasting romance."[3] Fondness is about liking or showing affection. Admiration is about respect and warm approval. Showing fondness and admiration to your partner lets them know you love them and are thinking about them.

You don't have to keep those positive thoughts to yourself. Tell your partner when you are proud of them or why you are attracted to them. Sometimes it may feel awkward to tell your partner those things out loud, or perhaps you think they should already know you love them and admire them. But I promise they will enjoy hearing you say, "I admire the way you..." or "I'm impressed that you..." You can also surprise your spouse by leaving fond or admiring notes on the bathroom mirror, in the car, by the coffee pot, or on their computer. It lets them know you are thinking about them.

Daily Rituals of Connection

Positive daily habits in marriage are crucial to the health of the relationship. Here are six rituals of connection I encourage my couples to incorporate into their daily lives.

Start the day off right

Consider starting your day by saying something positive when you greet your partner first thing in the morning. You could say, "Good morning!" or "How did you sleep?" Starting the day with criticism or complaints will only set a negative tone. Be positive when the day is starting and focus on greeting your partner with kind words. You can remind them of their responsibilities around the house some other time.

Decompress at the end of the day

I suggest what is called a "decompression time" when couples get home at the end of the day. The purpose of this ritual is to reconnect with your spouse and discuss external stresses from the day. Each of you takes ten to fifteen minutes to share what happened in your day. Listen intently to your partner to let them know you are interested and engaged. This is not the time to bring up relationship issues or for you to try to solve a problem for your spouse. This is a reconnecting time after being away from each other and a way to vent about the stresses of the day.

If necessary, to avoid distractions from children listening or interrupting, I suggest couples go outside to decompress or to a private area in the house. Teach your children the importance of this special "Mom and Dad time" by setting a boundary for them to not disturb you for twenty to thirty minutes.

Eat meals together

This may not always be possible, but try to have at least one meal each day when you are sitting down and eating together. It may be breakfast, or it can be a relaxing dinner in the evening when the distractions of cell phones and televisions are turned off.

Don't forget manners

Life is stressful, and when we are under pressure, manners are often the first thing to go. Say things more kindly than you think is necessary; say "thank you" and "please." Don't treat others in your life better than you do your spouse.

Forgive daily

When we pray the Lord's prayer, we ask God to "forgive us our sins, as we also forgive everyone who sins against us" (Luke 11:4, NIV). In marriage, this is a daily reminder to let go of any resentments you might be holding against your partner. It's hard to have a positive connection with your spouse when feelings of unforgiveness exist. Make it a daily ritual to forgive your spouse for any intentional or unintentional words or actions from the day. This will not only benefit your marriage—it will also benefit you personally.

Be affectionate

Holding hands, touching, kissing, or hugging can increase your relational connection. Make it a daily habit to be affectionate toward your partner. Not only is it good for your relationship, but it also releases oxytocin (the bonding hormone), which improves our mood and helps us be calm.

Coping with Stressors

Let's be honest, life is stressful. When you add a remarriage and stepfamily to the mix, life gets downright complicated. It's critical to have healthy ways of coping with stress so your marriage doesn't stay in a constant state of distress. Trouble begins when we start keeping things to ourselves and trying to deal with them on our own. Stress can pull you and your partner apart and impact how you communicate with each other and deal with conflict. Here are some ways to deal with stress.

Identify your stressors

Take some time to reflect on what in your life is causing you stress. Once you identify the stressors, discuss with your partner the following questions:

- How is stress impacting me?
- What are the healthy ways in which I'm coping?
- What are the unhealthy ways in which I'm coping?
- How is stress impacting my relationships?
- What can I do to reduce the stress?

Strengthen your resilience

Resilience is our ability to recover quickly from difficult situations like loss, tragedy, and trauma. The stronger our resilience, the better we cope with stressors that come our way. Here are some ways to increase your resilience:

- *Self-care*. Stress is hard on us psychologically and physically. Exercising, eating healthy, and having a positive outlook are great ways to improve mental health.
- *Social connection*. Connect with your partner and others. Find a social group that shares your interests and values.
- *Self-soothing*. When stress is high, take a break and breathe. Taking a walk or listening to your favorite music can be relaxing.

Couple Communication

As a couple, you must learn to communicate effectively, or conflict will destroy both your marriage and your new stepfamily. Here are some communication tips to keep your marriage on the path to success.

Talk and cooperate with your partner

It may seem silly to mention talking, but I've had couples in counseling who said they loved each other but didn't talk much. You have to talk if you are going to build a successful marriage and stepfamily. Some of your conversations will take place away from the children, but they will need to be part of the conversation when chores, schedules, or rules are being discussed.

Use your words

Speak up and say what you really need or want. If you want your spouse to just listen to you and not solve the problem, you could say, "Thank you for being so supportive. I need to vent about what happened at work today, but I don't need you to solve the problem—just listen."

Express your needs positively

It can be hard when you are hurting or frustrated to be careful with your words. However, if you verbally attack or criticize your spouse, he or she can become defensive. Once that happens, their active listening usually stops. Instead, try to find a way to connect positively with your partner. For example, instead of saying something like, "You're always working! Do you love the people at the office more than us?" try: "We have had some incredible vacations as a family, and I appreciate how hard you work for us. Is there a way you could take off for a few days of vacation so we can take the kids to our favorite camping spot? The whole family always seems to enjoy camping and fishing." Being noncritical and nonjudgmental changes the entire tone of the conversation.

Repair and restart

We all sometimes say things that we didn't intend to say, and occasionally we feel grumpy from having a bad day or not feeling well physically. When this happens, it's okay to ask for a "do-over." When you snap at someone, immediately repair the situation by saying, "Let me try that again in a nicer tone." Or if the negative conversation happened earlier, you could say, "I'm sorry I was grumpy this morning at breakfast. Can we have a new conversation about that subject?" It's always important to repair with kindness to your spouse and compassion for yourself.

Having Fun

Getting married and having a new stepfamily doesn't mean we have to stop having fun. Yes, there are more responsibilities and likely more conflicts between you and your spouse than when you were dating. However, it's vital to the marriage to have fun with your partner. Have a kids-free date night out, or carve out some one-on-one time at home with your spouse. One stepfamily I worked with became friends with another stepfamily in their church, and they would take turns watching each other's children so each couple could have a monthly date night. Also, don't spend your date night talking about problems. Remember, you are friends and lovers.

Another fun way to connect as a couple is to exercise. Research shows there are several benefits of exercising with your partner. One study revealed there is greater relationship satisfaction on the days you work out with your partner than when you work out alone.[4] The study also showed that we are more apt to stick with an exercise routine if we exercise with our partner. In addition to increasing marital satisfaction, exercising decreases cortisol (the stress hormone) and increases dopamine (the happy mood hormone).

Managing Conflict Successfully

Relationship expert John Gottman says, "It's not conflict itself that is the problem, but how we handle it."[5] Here are some helpful tips to manage marital conflicts.

Weekly check-ins

In his book *The Seven Principles for Making Marriage Work*, Gottman refers to weekly check-ins as "The State of the Union Meeting."[6] Whatever you decide to call it, scheduling a regular meeting to discuss and resolve small conflicts helps prevent them from growing bigger and helps to resolve minor problems so they don't keep surfacing throughout the week. When you know there will be a weekly constructive conflict discussion, you can think about what needs to be discussed and how you will address it. According to Gottman, there are three important sections to a conflict meeting:

1. **Warm-up.** Start the conversation by saying what you appreciate about each other. This sets a positive tone.

2. **Understanding.** This step is about listening to each of your perspectives on the issue. This is not the time to try to persuade your partner of your point of view. It's simply time to speak and listen.

3. **Compromise.** Now that you have heard each other's point of view, it's time to solve the problem together as a team. Brainstorm all the possibilities and come to a compromise so both of you get some of what you want, but neither gets all or none. If you can't come to an agreement, agree to table the matter and revisit it again the following week.

Take breaks if either of you starts feeling overwhelmed. If you are new to the weekly conflict meeting, ease into it by starting with a simple problem.

Discuss one issue at a time

Concentrate on solving one issue. If you try to resolve two problems at the same time, it will get overwhelming.

Don't use degrading language

No personal put-downs, swearing, or name-calling are allowed. Those tactics will only bury the original problem while making your partner feel bad. (It also will add to the list of things you need to discuss at your next weekly check-in.)

Use the "I" technique

This is a communication tool that focuses on what the speaker is feeling by using "I" statements instead of "you" statements, which can make listeners feel attacked. For example, you can say, "I feel unappreciated and taken for granted when I help your children with their homework every night while you watch television" instead of demanding, "You need to get up off the sofa and help your kids with their homework."

Take turns talking

Allow each person a minute to talk without being interrupted. Don't forget to listen to what your partner is saying instead of using his or her minute to think about what you are going to say.

Don't withdraw

Conflict can be hard; it's easy to retreat and refuse to speak. You might feel better in the moment as you withdraw, but it will cause more problems with your partner. If you feel overwhelmed, ask for a break and agree to resume later.

No yelling

Keeping your voices quiet and calm helps make discussion more constructive. Once you start yelling, the noise becomes the focal point instead of the issue.

Reaching Out for Support

The reality is, blending families is hard on relationships. Reach out to a couples' therapist if you need strategies or tools to improve your marriage. Many communities also offer support groups for stepfamilies. In addition, many churches now offer numerous small groups, Bible studies, and special events for stepparents. If you are unable to find a group, I encourage you to start your own. There are stepfamilies everywhere that need support.

Closing Thoughts from Steve

Misty and I did premarital counseling, read books to each other, and did what we knew to do before getting married. With all of that, we still had many struggles in our marriage. We immediately sought out the best help available. Each of us sees a counselor each week, and if there is a particular struggle we need help with, we will get help together. We believe in people getting counseling. Even greater than the number of couples who divorce is the number of people who are married but miserable. It is not a sign of weakness to hire a consultant for a business—and it is not a sign of weakness to hire a consultant for your marriage.

Key Points to Remember

- Have realistic expectations for your remarriage and stepfamily.
- A successful remarriage requires a foundation of trust, intimacy, fondness, and admiration.
- Positive daily habits in marriage are crucial to the health of the relationship.
- Adopt healthy ways of coping with stress.
- Learn to communicate effectively.
- Having fun with your partner is vital to your marriage.
- Learn skills to manage conflict successfully.
- Parenting in stepfamilies can be complicated. Reach out to a therapist or support group in your community to get additional help.

CHAPTER 5

Helping Children Manage Stress in the Blended Family

Rob and Kayla have been married less than two years. Kayla has a sixteen-year-old son and a fourteen-year-old daughter. Rob has a thirteen-year-old son. From the start, the three stepsiblings haven't gotten along. The two boys share a room and fight with each other daily. Rob's son often ends up in tears, and Kayla's daughter is anxious, trying to keep both her mom and dad happy. She tries not to mention Rob in front of her dad when she is with him on the weekends because he gets angry and insecure, asking her constantly which of them she loves more. When at home, Kayla's daughter is often irritable and lashes out disrespectfully toward both her mom and stepfather.

Rob is very concerned about Kayla's son being unkind and thinks they need to add another bedroom so each boy can have his own. Kayla disagrees; she says it's normal for teenagers to fight when sharing a bedroom and there is no real harm being done. Rob is frustrated because he thinks Kayla needs to discipline her children to be more respectful to all family members.

Understanding the Stresses

Parents and stepparents need to understand that adults and children experience stepfamilies very differently. So as adults, we need help to understand stepchildren's experiences and emotions.

To children, remarriage means changes in their lives that they didn't choose. They're adjusting to the new stepparents and also likely observing changes in their biological parents' attitudes toward each other. The children's level of stress also depends on which parent remarries, new expectations regarding visitation, changes in financial resources, stepsibling relationships, and sometimes a change of residence, school, or peer groups. Because of these new adjustments and stresses, some children withdraw to avoid family tension, while others may act out.

Since children may not be well acquainted with the stepparent at the time of remarriage, their opinion may be greatly impacted by the remarrying parent's former spouse, who may make negative comments concerning the new stepparent. Because children are forced to expand their family boundaries, they sometimes end up being messengers between their parents' households, creating even more stress.

The way parents and/or stepparents cope with that stress may directly influence the quality of family relationships, including setting the emotional tone of the household.[1] Research shows that children who have positive and consistent relationships with parents who model healthy coping skills during times of family stress are more satisfied in their stepfamily relationships. Further, researchers concluded that the daily stressors with the greatest impact on mood and health are often in the relationships themselves.

Grief and Other Emotions

Another couple, Sarah and John, came in for counseling because their thirteen-year-old son, Andrew, became withdrawn and surly after they announced they were separating. The moment he walked in the door after school, he would retreat to his room, and he rarely participated in dinnertime conversations. Both Sarah and John wanted to help Andrew face and process the big feelings he was dealing with, but they felt inadequate for the task.

Even though divorce is common in our society, few children are prepared for what it does to their family. Many children have no clue a divorce is coming; when they find out about it, they are shocked. Shock can be followed by denial, depression, and anger. Unfortunately, sometimes these effects can last several years. Sometimes parents try to ease the blow of divorce by telling their children about the separation ahead of time and explaining they are not divorcing the children. Even with that explanation, it is emotionally painful for the children, and these emotions can be very intense. Children have shared with me their anger and resentment about having no say in the decision. One twelve-year-old explained, "I was so angry when my dad moved out. My parents made this huge decision without asking any of us. My little brother slept in my bed every night for five months after Dad left. I had so much anger toward my parents as I held my brother, crying himself to sleep at night."

Children respond in different ways to a divorce. Preschool-age children often have the hardest time adjusting because they are not able to understand what is happening. All they know is that things look different in their family. Many times, preschoolers can be very clingy due to fears that both parents might abandon them. Regressive behaviors such as temper tantrums or bedwetting can also surface temporarily.

Children from six to nine sometimes feel like the divorce is their fault. They may respond by withdrawing from school-work and time with friends. As they get a little older, children may feel that they have to choose between their parents. This divided loyalty can lead to feelings of anxiety, shame, and stress.

Sometimes children will feel ashamed because they pre-fer the stepparent over their birth parent. Jake, Rob's thirteen-year-old son and Kayla's stepson, revealed in a ses-sion, "My real mom left us when I was eleven for another guy she met at work. My stepmom is really nice to me, and I really prefer to be with her. When my mom comes to pick me up on weekends, I have to avoid talking about my step-mom because my mom doesn't like her. I guess I love my mom, but I have a better relationship with my stepmom."

Teenagers experience pain and anger, too. Often, they may resort to rage and explosions. Sometimes they may focus their anger on a particular parent. Teenagers tend to understand better than their younger siblings why their parents have divorced. They realize they are not responsible for the divorce and look outside the home for support from friends, youth pastors, coaches, and teachers. It's still hard for teenagers to adjust, as noted by Kristine, Kayla's fourteen-year-old: "It was hard enough to try to learn to live alone with just my mom when my dad left us, but when she started dating, I had to have babysitters. It was like losing both parents in two years."

Stressful Adjustments

Not only do new emotions surface as children experience their parents' divorce, but many stressful adjustments in their new stepfamily's home life arise as well. Children have to learn to transition from a family where their biological parents lived together to alternating between their parents' homes. In addition, there is the adjustment to new stepparents and their likes, dislikes, and expectations. Problems can arise as children have to learn to abide by a new set of house rules and expectations from stepparents; accept discipline from a stepparent; be responsible for different chores and routines; develop stepsibling relationships; change school or friends; and sometimes adjust to new cultural and religious practices.

Children may not notice their own signs of stress. Often, physical signs of stress can be mistaken for illness. If you think your child is suffering from stress, it's a good idea to seek professional help.

Symptoms of Stress in Your Child

Physical Symptoms	Psychological Symptoms
Nausea	Nightmares or bad dreams
Stomachaches	Inability to concentrate
Nail biting	Problems at school
Tiredness	Forgetfulness
Headaches	Irritability
Increased or decreased appetite	Carelessness

Ways to Help Children Manage Stress

As a psychotherapist, I have found one of the best ways to help children with stress is to help the adults understand what their child needs. Here are some tools that will help reduce stepfamily stress for children.

Take things slowly

As we learned in the last chapter, it's crucial to take time to let everyone adjust to their new situation. Many couples rush into remarriage to avoid being single or because they want to be with their newfound love immediately. However, if they rush into things, not only do they avoid getting to know each other fully, but their children may have spent little to no time with their new stepparent. One stepdaughter shared, "I came home from school one afternoon to find a bunch of suitcases and boxes in the living room with my soon-to-be stepdad's clothes in them. I had no idea he was moving in. My mom never said a word to me or asked if it was okay."

Keep in mind, the relationship between the biological parent and children has existed longer than the relationship between the adults in the remarriage. The biological parent and their children have been emotionally bonded for years. On the other hand, the biological parent may have known her or his new partner for only a year, and although the children may like the stepparent, by comparison, they hardly know them.

Many times, adults move at a faster pace than the children need. Amazingly enough, it can take children longer to adjust to remarriage and being part of a stepfamily than to deal with their parents divorcing.[2] Additional research shows that the more change that happens in the remarriage and stepfamily, the more the children's well-being suffers.[3]

Let your relationship with your stepchildren develop gradually. Don't expect too much too soon, either from the children or yourself. Children need time to adjust, accept, and belong. So do parents. Resist the urge to rush into a relationship with your stepchildren.

It usually works best in the first year or two if you spend time being supportive of your stepchild, but not taking on an active parenting role. It's enough to be someone your stepchild can depend on to do the same things each week, like always taking him or her to a sporting event or outing on Saturdays. This will give your stepchild the chance to get to know and trust you.

Try to imagine what it would be like to be a child who has experienced his parents divorcing, remarrying, and having a stepfamily with new siblings, a new house, and new rules. Your bonus child is already going through many changes. Respect that he had a life before you entered it—a life that was erased by change he had no say in.

It's a bad idea to come into the stepfamily with a list of ways to "fix" things. If you do, your bonus kids might think you are trying to erase all evidence of their lives before you came along. Some examples would be trying to change the family's diet by eliminating sugar or suggesting the weekly tradition of going to the movies be changed to monthly. Give your new family a chance to become accustomed to each other and their new living arrangement. You can try to change one thing at a time by keeping in mind all family members will need to adjust and compromise. This includes you as well. Research shows it can take four to seven *years* for a stepfamily to function well as a family, so be patient and give everyone time.[4]

Accept and get to know your bonus child

The ideal situation is to get to know your stepchild before you marry her parent and start a new stepfamily. Be open and genuine. Kids have a way of knowing when you're being phony. Avoid the "let's sit down and get to know each other" approach, which usually isn't welcomed by teenagers and sometimes not by younger children either. Just make an effort to be around and be involved any chance you get. They'll let you know when the door is open.

Once that door is open, find time to spend one-on-one with your stepchild. This time can involve fishing, shooting hoops, playing catch, watching a favorite movie or show together, shopping, or other low-stress activities. You want to build the relationship through shared experiences that will give you opportunities to learn about each other. Try to choose an activity that neither of the biological parents do with the child to eliminate any appearance of competition. Consider practical things like helping your stepchild with homework or driving her to meet friends. Really get to know your bonus kids—who they are, what they're about, their likes and dislikes.

Rather than wishing your stepchild was different, accept his personality, habits, appearance, manners, behavior, style of dress, speech, choice of friends, and feelings—all of which you had nothing to do with. All children have positive qualities; identify those qualities and take advantage of opportunities to encourage them accordingly.

Stepparents can communicate acceptance of their stepchildren through verbal praise and positive or affectionate statements and gestures. I often share in counseling with the adults, "Everything you do or say either builds up or tears down the relationship with your bonus child." Be positive toward your stepchild. For example, you could point out when he does the right thing, or you could celebrate with a small surprise, like a trip to get his favorite treat, when your stepchild does well at something. Knowing and accepting the new child in your life will go a long way toward creating health in your new family.

As you get to know your bonus child, keep in mind that teenagers can be completely different than younger kids. To start off, there is puberty! Along with puberty are unwanted pimples, awkward growth spurts, and self-consciousness. Think about it: Would you want to go through puberty again?

Their new hormones are exploding. Those hormones rushing through their brains can provoke intense reactions. Expect vastly different moods in the same day—sometimes in the same hour. Remember that a teenager's main job is to learn how to become independent. They do this in the most annoying ways and can often get easily upset. So try not to take things personally. They are trying to manage and communicate their emotions all at the same time. Parents need to give them space, and stepparents need to give them more space. Expect them to communicate with grunts and eye rolls. If they react with intense anger, you can gently remind them to take a break, take a breath, and take time to get calm. Like anyone, they want to be heard. Hear them and give them space and time to adjust to you and their new stepfamily. If your step-teenager is having a particularly hard time, reach out to a counselor for help.

Support your child's relationship with the biological parent

Stepparents and ex-spouses should encourage children to have positive relationships with both biological parents. A continued relationship with both biological parents is crucial for the child to evolve into a healthy, emotionally adjusted adult. Encourage an environment in which he can love both of his parents. That continued relationship will help him manage his stress.

No matter what you think of your bonus child's other parent or how many times they have disappointed or failed your stepchild, they are still the child's mom or dad, and he or she loves them. Don't get me wrong, I'm not saying you can't have legitimate concerns about your stepchild's other parent. What I am urging is for you to exercise empathy and kindness for your stepchild. Please take my word for it: your bonus children will always need and seek the approval and love of both their biological parents.

Therefore, the worst thing you can do is talk badly about the other parent. I often remind my clients that it's kind of like when we were kids, and a bully called our little brother or sister a name. We wouldn't stand for it. Sometimes we would say mean things to our siblings, but if someone else said it, we got mad. So if a child is speaking in frustration about her biological parent, just listen. Maybe throw in a nod or two, but don't dare say an unkind word, or you will hear about it again.

One fifteen-year-old client shared her feelings about her stepmom's negative comments: "My stepmom says so many hurtful things about my mom. Each hateful word feels like acid in my heart. I don't think she realizes how badly her words hurt me." Even if your stepchild initiates negative conversations about her parent, just listen with empathy and decline to add to her put-downs.

Children of divorced families often struggle with what is called division of loyalties. This happens when children feel disloyal to one parent because of positive feelings for the other parent. Be sure to speak with your bonus children about their feelings and let them know it is okay to love their biological parents as well as a stepparent. It doesn't mean one will replace the other. One twelve-year-old boy remarked, "If I go to Disneyland or something like that with my stepdad, I don't tell my father, because I don't want him to feel bad for not taking me to places like that."

But we can help our children face this natural conflict. One father gently stated, "It must be very hard to have a mom and stepmom. Never forget you and your mom have a special bond because she gave birth to you. But I do hope one day you will begin to like your stepmom. When that time comes, it will be in a different place in your heart than your mom."

Implement one-on-one child-parent time

Children have a desire to deeply connect and bond with their biological parents. Set aside time as the parent to have regular one-on-one time with your biological children, without the stepparent. This time will help solidify your relationship and reduce the stress of the new family situation. It eases children's insecurities and fears regarding losing their parent to a new spouse, and establishes boundaries between parents, children, and the new couple. It is much easier for the children to accept the new marriage when they feel safe and secure in their bond with their biological parent. Research supports this, showing that positive parent-child relationships are linked to more positive stepparent-stepchild relationships.[5]

It's important that the stepparent understand this need and openly encourage this one-on-one time. Children often worry that a parent's love for the new spouse will mean less love for them. The children may be worried about the stepparent taking up all of their parent's time. They might long to have things like they used to be before the stepparent came along. This stress can cause children to behave with anger and resentment.

Help children identify their feelings

Children have a lot of big feelings. Their parents aren't together anymore, and they didn't ask for this new stepparent or new family. They are grieving in their own way, and very rarely do they know what to do with those feelings. Sometimes they will react and project their confusing emotions onto you.

An important task for adults is to give children a voice to express and process their feelings. Stepparents and parents can help children deal with their adjustments to their new life by helping them put a name to their feelings. Below is a sample of some feeling words:

List of Feelings

Happy	Sad	Angry	Other Feelings
Calm	Unhappy	Furious	Afraid
Silly	Withdrawn	Grumpy	Anxious
Loved	Hurt	Mad	Bored
Glad	Lonely	Mean	Confused
Content	Awful	Annoyed	Worried

A parent might say, "I wonder if you might be feeling anxious about not knowing when your dad will pick you up." Rob could ask his son, "How does it feel to share a room with someone? That must be hard when you don't know him very well."

Children should not be punished for expressing negative emotions toward stepfamily members. However, they should be encouraged to express emotions in productive and respectful ways. Children are more likely to accept their new stepfamily when adults invite them to share their feelings and concerns about their new family.[6]

Helping Children with Their Emotions

When children have strong emotions like disappointment, frustration, or rejection, it is difficult for them to express their feelings in healthy ways. And when divorce is part of their lives, emotions in children can be intense and sometimes explosive. This confuses them as well as the adults around them. Some parents and stepparents don't know how to help their children when they act out intense emotions by having a tantrum, screaming, or withdrawing. As the adults in their lives, we can help our kids develop coping skills to deal with their emotions in positive ways. Trying to reason or rationalize with children does not work when they are acting out due to intense emotions. Here are some ideas for adults to help.

1. **Help them identify what they are feeling.** Ask your child to share what is upsetting him. Once he talks about and can identify his feelings, he will begin to feel more in control of his emotions. A feelings chart (available online) can be very helpful in teaching kids to put a name to their feelings.

2. Look them in the eye. Get down on their level and look them in the eye as they tell you what is upsetting them. Children can tell when we are distracted or don't care.

3. Give them a safe environment to share. If other siblings or friends are around, this can inhibit true communication between you and the child. Go to a quiet place where it's only the two of you and there are no distractions.

4. Be supportive. Listen intently. Never ridicule a child.

5. Teach them deep breathing. When children are flooded with emotions, they may breathe shallowly. Teaching them to take slower and deeper breaths will help them to relax. Encourage them to breathe in through their noses and then breathe out through their mouths. Or breathe in for a few seconds, hold for a few seconds, and breathe out for the same number of seconds. One parent I saw in counseling carried a bottle of bubbles in her purse so that when her three-year-old started having a tantrum, the child could blow bubbles. This distraction also helped the child regulate her breathing.

6. Understand bodily symptoms of intense emotions. Be aware that sometimes intense emotions can show up in the form of a child's headaches, stomachaches, or withdrawn behavior. One stepmother noticed her eight-year-old step-daughter would have a stomachache when she was packing her suitcase to go back to her mother after spending the week-end with her dad.

7. Establish routines to help transitions. Transition times can be very stressful on children even if the parents are not fighting. Some children will have meltdowns during transition times, so rituals and routines are important to help smooth the way. Implementing routines can help everyone. One blended family I saw in counseling implemented the ritual of playing a funny CD while they were driving to exchange after a weekend visit with their mom. Another blended family would go to a nearby park to feed the ducks after exchanging children and let the kids run around and get out their pent-up energy from sitting in a car for several hours. Then they would get back in the car and drive another few hours to the other house. Once they arrived, they would put their weekend suit-cases in their rooms and play with the family dog while their stepmom and dad fixed their favorite pizza for supper. They did this every time, which made it easier for the children.

Acknowledging the stress your children may experience in a blended family is the first step toward health. With your acceptance, patience, and commitment, you and your spouse can create a home where children know they are accepted and loved, and feel safe to express their feelings.

Closing Thoughts from Steve

Before moving forward with blending a family, be sure to evaluate if you are ready. The kids need to know there are two adults in the room; you can't afford to act childish. If you are having a difficult time dealing with the stressors in your life, delay the marriage, especially if you are an individual who tends to take your stress out on other people or animals. There is no "taking things out on someone" in a healthy marriage. If you or your potential spouse do this, you both need to get good counseling before you move into marriage. You are not ready until anger is resolved and emotions are managed in a healthy way. Being or bringing someone who cannot handle stress to be part of the lives of your children is selfish, desperate, and unkind to kids who've had a tough enough time already.

Key Points to Remember

- Children experience stepfamily stresses differently than their parents do.
- Children experience intense emotions when their parents divorce.
- Parents can decrease stepfamily stress by taking things slowly, having realistic expectations,

having consistent family routines, and having one-on-one time with their own children.

- Much of stepchildren's stress comes from factors unique to remarried families, including conflicting loyalties, stepsiblings, and learning to get along with their stepparents.
- Stepparents need to leave the discipline to the biological parent, yet maintain accountability and require respectful interaction from the stepchildren.
- It's important for stepparents and parents to encourage children to have positive relationships with both biological parents, eliminating loyalty conflicts for the children. Never openly criticize the ex-spouse.
- Children and adults need to learn positive coping skills to deal with stress on a daily basis.

CHAPTER 6

Conquering Difficulties

Yolanda's face was reddening as she vented in my counseling office one afternoon. "When I married Hector, I didn't realize how much his ex-spouse, Maria, would be in our lives. I knew his two children were an all-in-one kind of bundle, but I never dreamed Maria was part of the bundle! I need help dealing with her controlling issues with Hector—and now she's trying to control me."

Exes Are Part of the New Stepfamily

Starting a new stepfamily can be a time for hopeful new beginnings. But along with the new beginning comes the past. Former spouses must learn to coparent their children together, and as a stepparent, you now have a role to play as well. Difficulties with exes will arise but can be alleviated by accepting the reality that they are part of the family. The most important part is learning how to deal with the intense emotions that surface when trying to raise the children together. Many difficulties in stepfamilies can drive intense emotions in all the adults involved in the children's lives. Moms, dads, stepmoms, and stepdads have to learn to control their responses and emotions, because those responses can impact everyone.

Moms, stepmoms, dads, and stepdads

Yolanda and Maria were capable of causing major conflict in both of their families. Bonus moms fear being called a "wicked stepmother," whereas moms might fear they will lose their children to the new wife. It's imperative that moms and stepmoms learn to manage these fears and make room for each other, or they will make everyone suffer. Conflict of any kind is not healthy for the children.

Dads and stepdads appear to have an easier time getting along compared to moms and stepmoms. Research shows most stepchildren have a good relationship with both their biological father and their stepfather. There is a significant positive association between the quality of relationships with stepfathers and children's stepfamily adjustments and well-being. Relationships with noncustodial fathers are less consistent but appear to have positive effects on children's adjustments to the stepfamily.[1]

Conflict Research

According to the *International Handbook of Stepfamilies*, children's well-being is determined by the quality of the parenting practices and the family's level of conflict.[2] Some family scholars and researchers believe conflict is the main predictor of children's well-being after divorce.[3] Research also concludes that if children are continually exposed to conflict, it impacts their ability to control their own emotions.[4] In addition, research conducted over a span of thirty years shows that moderate conflict negatively influences children's self-esteem, social and cognitive abilities, academic achievement, and romantic relationships.[5] This damage from conflict continues after the children leave the home.[6] Therefore, it's extremely important to find ways to reduce conflict within the blended family in order for the children to have a positive experience with the new adjustments.

Positive coparenting

The preferred method to maintain a low level of conflict is positive coparenting. This is achieved through frequent communication, solving problems without letting emotions get out of hand, and working toward compromise.[7] If positive coparenting is not possible, the next best thing is what is called "low-conflict parallel parents." This term was coined by Jan Pryor, a psychology professor at Victoria University in Canada and director of the Roy McKenzie Centre for the Study of Families. Pryor defines "low-conflict parallel parents" as divorced parents who are "running their households quite separately from each other."[8] Parallel parenting allows them to remain disengaged and limit direct contact with each other for all but the most critical decisions. For example, the parents will make school and medical decisions together, but the day-to-day decisions will be made separately.

The key to being successful in both co-parenting and parallel parenting is to keep the focus on the children. In the end, to the extent possible, you want your children to see their parents working together for their well-being. This allows your children to observe good communication and problem-solving skills, which will help them later on in life.

Communication

In order to communicate well in a way that does not impact the kids negatively, coparents need to communicate directly with each other. In my counseling practice, I remind clients not to use their children to send messages to their former spouse. Some have said they are trying to avoid a negative confrontation or conflicted communication with their ex, so they have the kids deliver the message. However, this causes pain and anxiety for the children. One child shared with me during a counseling session, "My mom would tell me to ask dad why he hasn't paid his child support this month. I hated when my mom put me in the middle like this. It wasn't until my teen years that I had the courage to tell my mom she needed to talk to dad about money and quit using me as her messenger. She was mad at first, but then she started talking to my dad more and they resolved it. I hated being the go-between."

You do not need to share with your children all the details of what is going on between you and their other parent. You can tell them things like, "We can either go miniature golfing or out for pizza, but we cannot do both," rather than saying you could do more fun things if the other parent paid more child support. When you are angry at your ex-spouse, vent to your adult friends or your therapist, not your children. And be aware that little ears hear every conversation, whether in person or on phone calls. Many a child has been caught eavesdropping in stairways, around corners, or at closed doors.

Transition times

When parents exchange children for their scheduled visits, it's vital to be calm and peaceful. Transitions can cause emotional responses in children. If there is conflict between the parents, children's anxiety and fear can increase. I counseled a nine-year-old girl whose mom brought her in after her pediatrician said her frequent stomachaches were caused by anxiety. "When it was our weekend to go to my dad's house, my mom would always be late," she said. "Sometimes she would be several hours late to meet him, and he would sit there waiting for her. I immediately would get sick to my stomach, knowing dad was waiting for hours—and what if there was an argument once we got there? Once I threw up in the car because my stomach hurt so badly, and that made us even later."

Don't use the transition time to discuss things that are bothering you or any other issues. The kids do not need to hear it. Talk about those things another time when the children are not present.

Different household rules

Respect each household's rules even if you disagree, especially in front of the children. When a child says he gets to stay up until midnight on weekends at the other parent's house, you can reply softly and calmly, "Yes, at your dad's your bedtime is midnight, but here it is nine p.m. Once you get older, we can discuss a different bedtime." Most children can handle the different rules at each house as long as their parents aren't fighting over them.

Don't make plans with the kids on the ex-spouse's weekend unless you discuss it with the other parent and they agree to it. Schedule changes need to be fair to both parents. I suggest that if parents cannot come to a compromise, then the original schedule stays. And be sure the focus stays on the child's performances, school activities, graduations, weddings, etc.—not the adults' agendas. In some cases, I've encouraged clients to sit far away from their ex-spouses at the kids' events because of conflict, or to arrive at different times to avoid walking in together.

How to Deal with Difficult Emotions

Let's face it. Being in a stepfamily is hard. Emotions can get the best of you. On any given day, things can be going well and then BANG! Anyone can say or do something that sets you off. Your response can be impacted by your frame of mind or the circumstances surrounding the situation. It's helpful to discover ways to deal with your own intense feelings as well as how to help your children and stepchildren do the same.

Recognize your feelings

Every day we experience all kinds of emotions: annoyance, anger, joy, disappointment, excitement, shame, or rejection. Situations common to stepfamilies, like talking to your spouse about the kids, asking your stepchildren to do something, or seeing your spouse's ex act a certain way, can exacerbate existing emotions.

Events, experiences, or memories from our past can trigger us to react with emotional intensity. In stepfamilies, both adults and children have gone through trauma from a divorce. Here are a few emotional triggers that have been shared in my office:

- Being ignored by a spouse or stepchild
- Feeling rejected or not included
- Fear of being abandoned
- Feeling unwanted
- Feeling unworthy or not good enough
- Feeling ugly
- Feeling insecure

In addition to identifying your feelings, recognize what your body is doing during these intense times. Sometimes you can be breathing fast, sweating, or having racing thoughts, upset stomach, or pounding heart.

Once you recognize these signs, try to trace the feeling back to where it started and what caused it. See if there is any connection to a feeling from the past that triggered the same feeling in a similar situation. For example, Yolanda, who had issues with her husband's ex, Maria, said, "When Maria started being controlling of me as far as giving me a list of what the kids should wear when they were at our house, and what foods she allowed them to eat, my emotions went vertical! Who does she think she is to tell me what to fix her kids to eat and when they should wear certain clothes? My feelings were anger, annoyance, hostility, and fear. I remember feeling like this when my mom would be controlling of me growing up, and it drove me crazy! I couldn't wear certain outfits to school if they weren't on the schedule. And I never was allowed any kind of sugar or candy in the house, even on Halloween. I had to donate my Halloween candy to the neighbor kids across the street."

Yolanda was able to see the connection between her intense feelings and events from her past, when her mother had been controlling. When she recognized the trigger that caused her emotional pain, she could choose a different response by talking to Maria about her concerns.

Often a triggering event like Yolanda's can bring about negative thoughts, which in turn cause an emotional response. But as Yolanda learned to respond instead of react, she was able to gain more control of her own feelings and the situation.

Manage your feelings in the moment

Here are some ideas to help you manage your feelings in the moment instead of reacting to the trigger.

1. **Recognize your warning signs before your emotions get the best of you.** Did you have a bad day at work? Are you hungry? How much sleep did you get last night? For example, if you notice you are irritable when you are hungry, wait to discuss things until you've eaten.

2. **Give yourself permission to take a short break.** Once you give yourself some space, try some deep breathing or reframing what just happened. Once you feel relaxed, return to the situation with your emotions calmer.

3. **Think before you speak.** In an emotionally charged conversation, take a deep breath and listen very carefully to the other person. This gives you the opportunity to reflect on what the other person is saying before you speak.

4. **Consider the others person's point of view.** Perhaps the person who has upset you is dealing with their own triggers. Most people don't purposefully try to upset us. I'm not sure who said it, but one of my favorite sayings I share with my clients in

counseling is, "99 percent of how people respond to you has nothing to do with you." What does this mean? It means that at any given moment, everyone has many emotions going on inside that others are not aware of. So try to consider others' perspectives. You may not agree with them, but at least consider them.

5. Focus on relaxing. You can relax in the moment by thinking about a memory that calms you. Maybe it's a favorite vacation or a favorite memory with a loved one. Many clients say that imagining being out in nature is very calming. Envision yourself as a person who is in control of his emotions and able to resolve this situation.

6. Get plenty of exercise and sleep. Many of my patients forget about the impact exercise and sleep have on how we handle difficulties. Exercising helps get rid of tension that can cause emotional flare-ups. Walking outside gives us fresh air to breathe and can give us a different perspective on a problem. Getting enough sleep is important, as it helps us better regulate our emotions.

7. Leave the past behind. This is easier said than done. However, forgiving yourself and the other person for past mistakes is important so they don't get in the way of you trying to solve the current problem.

8. Communicate using "I" or "me" statements. When someone triggers your emotions, take a deep breath and communicate what you are feeling. For example, instead of telling Maria, "You can't tell me what to do in my own house!" Yolanda could have calmly tried saying, "Can you share with me specifically your concerns about the food we eat at our house?"

9. **Imagine someone you admire handling the situation.** Think about someone you look up to and how they would advise you to handle the situation. Or you could ask yourself how they would handle the situation if it was happening to them.

10. **Build a buffer when you notice an emotional trend.** Give yourself a few extra minutes when you foresee a tense emotional situation. If you are meeting your ex-spouse to exchange the kids for the weekend, arrive early so you can do some deep breathing and imagine how you might handle different scenarios that may arise. One of my patients shared that she soaks in a hot tub an hour before she and her ex exchange their kids. She feels relaxed and more in control of her emotions when the meeting happens.

11. **Accept the reality of the situation.** Stepparenting and coparenting with an ex-spouse is hard work. Don't expect everything to be roses. We cannot control the stressors that come into our lives, but we can control how we respond to those stressors.

Continual Healing for Difficult Emotions

Managing feelings in the moment is very helpful, but sometimes we may need to dig deeper to figure out why our emotions are so intense. Examining root causes will help emotions to be less intense over time. Here are some ideas for long-term healing.

1. **Explore cognitive behavioral techniques.** These help people learn how to identify and change destructive thought patterns that have a negative influence on behavior and emotions. They work wonders on helping you understand how you process thoughts and feelings. When it comes to intense emotions and responses, they can be very helpful.

2. **Try mindfulness.** Practicing mindfulness allows you to be more in tune with how you feel in the present moment. It can help you recognize your triggers, and then you can decide how to deal with them.

3. **Keep a feelings journal.** Once you've mastered mindfulness, try keeping a log of the different feelings you have throughout the day. This can help you recognize a variety of emotions and help you see the patterns of your triggers. Once you see the patterns, you can choose to respond differently in the future when those types of feelings show up. For example, instead of blowing up or shutting down when someone makes

you angry, you can choose to have a calm conversation with that person.

4. Find a counselor/therapist. Managing our emotions can be difficult by ourselves at first. And sometimes we don't see some of our own emotional triggers right away. Therapy will give you a safe place to share your feelings and explore what may be causing some of your triggers.

5. Manage your automatic negative thoughts (ANTs). Dr. Daniel Amen coined the term ANTs in his book *Change Your Brain, Change Your Life.*[9] ANTs can ruin your day, steal your joy, and prolong grief. Here are some negative thoughts you might have:

"My spouse's ex is ruining my life."

"My spouse will never stand up to his/her ex, so my life will be horrible."

"My stepchildren will never respect me."

"I can't take this anymore!"

"Nothing will ever change."

According to Dr. Amen, we have to challenge these negative thoughts and replace them with the truth. Here are the truths that can replace the negative thoughts above:

"My spouse's ex cannot ruin my life. He or she can make it uncomfortable, but only I can choose if my life will be ruined or not."

"Even if my husband or wife chooses not to stand up to his or her ex-spouse, this does not mean I cannot set my own healthy boundaries with this person."

"Being a stepparent is hard, and it's hard for kids to have a stepparent. This will take time, but eventually they may respect me. If they don't, I can set healthy boundaries on what I will and will not allow. My happiness is not based on what they do."

"This is uncomfortable, but it's not the end of the world. I can handle it."

"Some things will take longer to change. However, if things do not change, I can choose to still have joy and enjoy other things in my life."

Closing Thoughts from Steve

In this chapter, everything is included that needs to be done to coparent the best way possible, whether or not your spouse's ex is healthy and cooperative. We've included two comprehensive lists that provide the path out of constant conflict and into a peaceful way of life absent anyone inflicting pain on anyone else and regret piling on top of regret. Knowing how to do these things is just the first half of transforming yourself into a mature adult who can manage emotions rather than inflict pain on others; the second half is doing what it takes. You must want the problem to be resolved, and you must want to change. If you find yourself stuck because you are not willing to do anything to get better, it is time to confess this to your potential spouse; otherwise, you'll hurt everyone involved.

In a world where reacting, rather than responding as an adult, is quite common, you can be the adult anywhere you need to coparent. Being in control feels good compared to being controlled by someone who knows which buttons to push to set you off into a childish rant or quick disconnection. There is a little-known mindset that can help you avoid being triggered by a very unhealthy person: amused detachment.

Rather than becoming triggered by a person doing what they do predictably over and over again, we can instead decide to be amused by the repeated routine. When they look like they want to stir up conflict, you don't engage and fight back. Instead you detach, becoming an observer rather than a victim. It is almost like an out-of-body experience. You see beyond the words and manipulation of the other and are actually amused by it. You keep yourself detached and calm while seeing them bait you and become frustrated because you won't be hooked into their negative way of being. When you do this, you win and your bonus kids win.

You win because you are in control and feel good about rising above the fray. Your kids also win when they see you model not falling prey to someone else's predictable defective strategies. And the more you see it, the more amused by it you become.

This might be the only time detachment is a healthy thing. Try it. You will like being the wise observer more than playing the role of the weak person hooked into a conflict you cannot win.

Key Points to Remember

- Exes will always be part of the family.
- Children's well-being is determined by the level of conflict between the coparents.
- Coparents need to communicate directly with each other and not through the children.
- Don't leak information to your children about their other parent. Children do not need all the details about what goes on between the two of you.
- When exchanging children with the coparent, the transitions should be calm and peaceful.
- Respect each parent's household rules even if you disagree, especially in front of the children.

- Learn to deal with your own intense feelings before you help your children or stepchildren do the same.
- If you or your children are struggling with intense emotions, seek professional counseling to learn healthy ways to express feelings.

CHAPTER 7

Healthy Communication in Stepfamilies

With tears starting, thirteen-year-old Jasmine blurted out, "Oh, Dad!" as he stepped closer and put his arm around her shoulder. "You have no idea what it's like to be the new kid in school and not have anyone to sit with during lunch. Why did we have to move into a new school district after you married Trisha?"

"No, sweetheart, I don't know what it's like," her dad said softly. "It must feel lonely and terrible."

"It does! No one wants to be my friend. I've tried smiling, talking, and being friendly. Every night I dread going back to school the next day."

Good communication skills are vital for keeping stepfamilies strong. When comparing stepfamilies that thrive with those that struggle, it's obvious that the thriving stepfamilies have adopted healthy communication skills.[1]

In this chapter we'll discuss communication patterns that build connection and intimacy in stepfamilies. We will also discuss negative communication patterns that damage relationships. Psychologist and author Patricia Papernow stresses the importance of "connection before correction." She encourages stepparents to focus on empathetic listening, expressing warmth and caring, and practicing constructive communication.[2] For example, if a child says to her dad, "I hate my stepmother," what the child needs most is a response like, "It must be very frustrating to have a new parent." Empathy is often the key to helping the child who is struggling. It's about connecting with your child in the midst of a very hard and emotional transition. Then shift to constructive communication by saying something like, "Specifically what is it that makes you hate your stepmother? Is it frustration with the situation, something she does, or what?" As the parent, you continue the process of going back and forth between empathetic listening and constructive communication until your child feels heard and knows you care.

Being Available to Your Children

In order to communicate with your children, you need to be there. I often tell parents to simply be available in case their children want to talk. Be there to simply listen when they have concerns or fears. Ask them on a daily basis about what's happening in their lives. This will give you clues about changes that may be causing them stress or worry. Researchers say there are several communication behaviors that build successful stepparent-stepchild relationships: active listening, open and flexible communication, using constructive conflict management skills, offering praise, and expressing empathy, as well as other non-intrusive caring behaviors.[3] Let's look at each of these in turn.

Active listening

Listening is so basic that we often don't think about whether we are doing it successfully. However, most people need to work on their active listening skills; it is the key to greater understanding. Here are some tips for listening better:

- Focus on what the person is saying. Don't try to do something else at the same time, like looking at your phone or computer while he or she is talking. Give that person your undivided attention.
- Listen intently without planning what you are going to say once they stop talking.

- Keep quiet until they are finished. When they finish, verbally summarize what you heard them say and ask if you got it right.
- Ask questions if you don't understand or need more information.
- Avoid finishing the speaker's sentences.
- Just listen; don't offer up a solution or advice.
- Be careful not to take something negative they might say personally. This will cause you to get defensive and not listen to what they are saying.

When conflict exists, we often become defensive, and listening may be forgotten as we try to get our point across to the other person. Here are some ways to help keep your emotions in check while listening:

1. **Breathe slowly.** Taking slow, deep breaths and letting them out slowly is a great way to remain calm during the conversation.

2. **Remind yourself that you love this person.** It's important to get your hurts out of the way and focus on your love for the other person. Focus on trying to understand their pain.

3. **Take notes about the conversation.** This will keep you from getting defensive and help you be accurate when it's your turn to talk.

4. It's okay to pause. If you feel your emotions are too intense or you are having a hard time listening, say you need a break. You could say something like, "I'm having a hard time listening right now because I'm taking things you say very personally. Can we take a break and start again in twenty minutes?"

Open and flexible communication

Parents and stepparents need to be as direct and open as possible with their children and stepchildren when communicating. It's important to model being transparent, authentic, and honest about how you feel. And yet, it's important to remember to be kind and not hurtful. Open and flexible communication is never intentionally mean or hurtful.

Constructive conflict management skills

How stepfamilies communicate about disagreements, rather than the mere presence of disagreements, is the key to their mental health.[4] Here are some guidelines for conflict management within the blended family:

1. **Use "I" statements to avoid attacks.** Attacks are verbal assaults on a person's character or self-esteem. John Gottman stresses that nasty remarks or insults are destructive when trying to resolve issues, so we must avoid them.[5] Try to use

"I" rather than "you" or "why," because the two latter words can be perceived as attacks by the listener. For example, instead of asking your stepchild, "Why do you always use my tools and never put them back?" you could make the statement, "I'm irritated that my tools are outside in the grass instead of back in my tool chest. I expect my tools to be returned to the tool chest after they are borrowed." This statement will allow for further communication to take place. The "I" statement expresses the parent's feelings of irritation and the expectation. The message comes across, but it's not filled with hurtful words as it might be otherwise.

2. **Time and place matter.** Discussions are often not constructive if they are raised at the wrong time. One person may be ready to talk, whereas the other person may be tired or distracted. If possible, decide on a time and place to have your discussion. This allows both parties time to organize their thoughts and control their emotions, which may increase the chance of the discussion going in a positive direction.

3. **Stay focused.** Conflict management aims to solve a specific problem. It's easy to bring up other issues during a discussion, but don't pile in all the other frustrations you've been carrying around. Often the person listening will feel overwhelmed if there are too many issues on the table. Be specific about what you would like your partner or stepchild

to do about the problem you are bringing up. For example, saying, "I feel very frustrated with you right now" doesn't give the person a specific behavior you would like them to change. Instead, you could say, "Several weeks ago when we discussed what chore you would be taking on, you chose to put the trash out by the curb on Tuesday mornings before school. This is the second week in a row that you have forgotten. I think it would be better if you put the trash out the night before since mornings are pretty busy trying to get ready for school." The second statement gives the recipient something specific to do to help solve the problem you have raised.

4. **Don't try to win.** When there is a conflict, it's not about who wins and who loses. Family members should not compete during a conflict to establish one loser and one winner. When this happens, the loser becomes resentful, and it hurts the relationship. And of course, this means it really is a "lose-lose" conflict because in the end the relationship is damaged. To avoid this damage, it's helpful to embrace the perspective that if I am "against" you, my focus is on myself. Instead of focusing on yourself, focus on the love you have for your child or partner. This helps you look beyond yourself. The conflict can be a situation where you see compromise as a way to grow, listen more, and seek to better understand your child or partner. It's also helpful if you accept the reality that every

situation can have two very valid perspectives: yours and the other person's. No one perspective is right or wrong. An exercise I use with clients for solving a conflict is getting them to imagine the problem is sitting on a table in front of them. Their challenge is to try to detach from the problem and try to solve it as a team.

5. **Avoid triggers.** Triggers are memories, experiences, or events that can cause intense emotions. For example, a person may get angry when they think someone is telling them what to do, which stems from how they felt when they were controlled in the past. We all have triggers like these, and most of the time they can make a conflict worse and more intense. Usually we know what our child's or partner's triggers are; if you don't, have an honest conversation to find out what they might be. Be aware of those triggers and protect your loved one by showing compassion and not bringing them up during a conflict.

6. **Turn criticisms into wishes.** It is easy to share what we are unhappy about in the form of a criticism. However, criticisms will make the person listening become defensive and try to protect themselves. When we are focused on being defensive, we are not in the frame of mind to solve a problem. Turning your criticism into a wish will help focus the conversation on what you want and what you need. For example,

instead of "I hate when I drive up to the house and see your bicycle in the driveway where I need to park," turn the criticism into a wish: "I would like for your bike to be parked in the garage and not in the driveway."

Offering praise

When you see good qualities in your children or partner, tell them what you like about them. Actively look for the good in all your family members and give them sincere compliments. Praise their attempts to do something right, even if they fail. Focus on their strengths and build them up; that will help the relationship. People will improve when you praise them.

If you overlook the things you don't like and focus on the things you do like, it will change the atmosphere in your home and improve your relationships. Proverbs 27:17 says, "As iron sharpens iron, so a friend sharpens a friend" (NLT). Don't use your iron (words) to bring someone down; use them to build them up. Everything we say or do is either building up the relationship or tearing it down. Use your iron to encourage and motivate your children and partner when you see them doing right.

Expressing empathy

Empathy is generally understood as *the ability to identify and share someone else's emotions and experiences.* Empathy is when you let your children or partner know that their feelings are both heard and understood. Being empathetic is giving your loved one attention, affection, or support. Empathy is letting your loved one know you are interested in them, you hear them, and you accept them.

Here are some examples of showing empathy:

- You listen quietly and give the person your full attention.
- You acknowledge their comments.
- You give their feeling a name. "How irritating!"
- You let them know you wish you could give them what they need. "I wish I could make your stomachache go away."

Other non-intrusive caring behaviors

In addition to the abovementioned skills that are vital for healthy stepfamily communication, here are some other things to consider in your conversations.

1. **Tone of voice.** This is a small part of communication, but we shouldn't underestimate it. Improving your tone during a conflict or in everyday conversations will help create a positive atmosphere and strengthen your relationship with your family. Your tone clarifies and gives meaning. A phrase as

simple as "Oh, really?" can be taken in different ways depending on how you say it. And if your tone is negative, there's a good chance people may not be willing to listen to your message.

Sometimes your tone may be sharp or loud because you are feeling stressed. Before starting a conversation, take time to reflect on how you are feeling and delay the conversation if necessary. When working with patients who struggle with their tone, I ask them to record themselves so they can learn how they come across when speaking to others. Most are unaware.

2. The 5:1 ratio. Relationship expert John Gottman has found that people are the happiest when positive interactions outweigh negative interactions in the ratio of 5:1—meaning they have five positive ones for every negative one.[6] This also applies to parent-child and stepparent-child relationships.

3. The soft/hard/soft technique. This was coined by stepfamily expert Patricia Papernow.[7] When a difficult conversation needs to take place, use this technique to make it more kind and loving: Start with something kind or positive, bring up the "difficult" topic in a soft way, then end with another kind or positive statement.

For example, let's revisit the conversation between Jasmine and her dad at the beginning of this chapter. The soft statements are in bold. Notice that they are at the beginning and end, and the hard statements are sandwiched in between.

Dad: "**Sometimes this new family and new school are a lot of changes to deal with at one time for you.** But you're getting older now and even though it's uncomfortable at first, you will hang in there because you know making new friends will happen as the school year progresses and you get involved with after-school activities. **I love you and I'm here to help you get through this.**"

4. Words matter; be kind. Bestselling Christian author Lysa TerKeurst challenged her social media followers to realize the power of words when she tweeted, "Oh, friend… let's remember that words are never just syllables and nouns. They can be blessings or burdens. The words we let loose into the world cause people to either celebrate or suffer. Our choice."[8]

Improving Communication with Your Children

We've mentioned several times that being a child of divorce is hard, and those kids often feel confused, frustrated, and angry. As their parent or stepparent, you can model healthy communication skills. Let them know you are interested in them by how you communicate with them. Helping them deal with their feelings, engaging their cooperation, encouraging their autonomy, using praise and building their self-esteem, avoiding "dead-end" questions, and seeking apologies and repairs to damaged aspects of the relationship are all good strategies for improving communication in the blended family.

Helping children deal with their feelings

Children need to have their feelings heard and accepted. You can help by listening quietly and tuning in to what they are saying. You can acknowledge what they are saying by putting their feelings into a word or two. For example: "That sounds overwhelming!" Even when you acknowledge that their feelings are heard and accepted, you can emphasize that certain actions are not. For example, "I can see how frustrated you are with your stepsister for borrowing your things without asking, but instead of shoving her, tell her what you want in words."

Engaging children's cooperation

State the facts and describe what the problem is. "You have clothes and shoes on the floor in the bathroom." Then give information and encourage their cooperation to solve the problem. "I am having friends over tonight for dinner and that is the bathroom guests will use when they are visiting."

Encouraging autonomy

Let children make age-appropriate choices such as, "Do you want to wear pants or a skirt today?" Don't always rush in to give the answer for them. For example, if your child asks you for ideas on a science fair project, you could say, "That's a tough one! What part of science is your favorite?" Encourage children to use resources outside the house: "You might go to the library and see if they have a book on science fair projects."

Using praise and building their self-esteem

Instead of just observing and noting to yourself what your child has done, describe what you see, such as, "I noticed you put away your bicycle in the garage," or "It's great to come home and see your chores have been done!" You can also sum up what the child has done with praise words: "The shoes in your closet look great! That's what I call organization!"

Avoiding dead-end questions

If you ask simple questions, you're going to get simple answers. Try to avoid "yes" and "no" questions, as these can end conversations before they even get started. If you ask, "How are you?" your child can answer, "Fine." So ask more open-ended questions like, "What are you excited about right now?" or "What was your favorite part of school today?"

Seeking apologies and repairing damaged aspects of the relationship

No matter how careful we try to be, we are occasionally going to say something hurtful or mean, raise our voices, or get defensive. In healthy relationships, when this happens, it's important to repair those interactions as soon as possible and to realize that the relationship is way more important than the problem. The right repairs can heal the relationship and put it back on the path of intimacy and closeness. Here are some healing repair statements:

"I didn't mean that the way it came out. Let me try it again."

"I'm sorry I hurt your feelings. I love you."

"I can tell I have hurt you. What can I do to make things better?"

"Can we take a break and try this again in twenty minutes? My emotions are all over the place."

"We may not come to an agreement on this. Can we agree to disagree?"

"What you said hurt my feelings. Can you say it in a different way?"

"I need you to forgive me for what I said."

Communication Killers to Avoid

Some unsuccessful types of communication that have a tendency to alienate people can be anger, conflict avoidance and stonewalling, mixed messages, passive-aggressive behavior, criticism, contempt, and defensiveness.

Anger

Uncontrolled anger by yelling or being verbally abusive immediately shuts down communication. If an angry person says the first thing that comes to mind, it's usually very hurtful or unkind. If you feel yourself getting really angry, step away to cool down before finishing the conversation. Resentment and shutting down often is a result of people witnessing explosive anger.

Conflict avoidance and stonewalling

Clients I've seen in counseling often share that they avoid conflict because they don't want to hurt their partner or child. Often, however, it's really themselves they are trying to protect. They are trying to protect themselves from feeling their own pain, fear, shame, or embarrassment. Sometimes, conflict avoiders will leave the house when a fight threatens or refuse to argue or talk. In the end it makes everyone feel worse, not better. When people refuse to communicate and instead shut down, the relationship becomes fragile.

Mixed messages

Mixed messages are those given at the same time that contradict each other. These confusing messages can both be verbal, or one can be verbal and the other nonverbal. For example, a family member may agree to go to a movie, but at the same time say they are tired. Some people give the "silent treatment" when they continue to say nothing is wrong. These kind of mixed messages create distance and cause pain and confusion in relationships.

Passive-aggressive behavior

When a person expresses anger at someone but does so indirectly, that is known as passive-aggressive behavior. People use passive aggression because they are afraid of direct conflict. Criticism, nagging, and sarcasm are all forms of passive-aggressive behavior. This kind of behavior causes distance and pain in the relationship.

Criticism

Criticism is when we attack our child's or partner's personality or character rather than focusing on the real issue that is bothering us. You could be direct and say, "I wish you would call if you are going to be late for dinner" instead of being critical and saying, "You are so rude and inconsiderate when you show up whenever you want for dinner."

Contempt

Contempt is an obvious sign of disrespect. It can involve insults, name calling, and nonverbal signs such as rolling eyes or smirking. Even using humor in a hurtful way is a sign of contempt.

Defensiveness

When a person feels criticized or emotionally injured by another, he can become defensive. This in turn can cause him to not take responsibility for his actions or deal with the issue that is being discussed. The relationship declines when one party is making excuses or denying responsibility.

Communication with the "Other" Family

We have discussed how to have healthy communication among stepfamily members. However, I want to briefly mention the importance of healthy communication with ex-spouses. This can be hard because sometimes there are still intense emotions of jealousy, anger, or sadness coming from both directions that get in the way of healthy communication. One method that helps when communication is difficult between the two families is what is called "Dutch door."[9] A Dutch door is a door that is divided so the bottom half may remain shut while the top half opens. In this communication technique, the bottom part of the door is the private information about the parents' personal lives that doesn't have anything to do with coparenting the children. This part of the door stays shut. The top part of the door stays open for discussions only about coparenting issues like children's after-school activities or vacations. In other words, you only discuss things that have to do with coparenting your children. This is not a perfect technique but can definitely help with stressful communication.

Closing Thoughts from Steve

When it comes to the best practices for communication, I need all of the assists I can get. To that end, I developed some rhyming opposites to help me stay on my side of the street after my divorce, focusing on what I could do rather than demanding or expecting something from a person who was committed to not doing anything someone else wants. Here they are:

Don't lecture; actively listen. Why waste energy spilling a bunch of words out of your mouth that have no meaning or worth to the other person? Instead, listen deeply for inroads into their heart and soul. Most resistant people will unknowingly reveal the path you can take to connect and communicate.

Don't disconnect; offer respect. People don't become damaged on accident. Beneath the problem is a person who has been hurt and wounded. Offering a bit of respect for them as a human being tends to increase the likelihood of compliance or at least the greatest chance for civility.

Don't repudiate; validate. Most likely this person has been rejected by others. They have probably suffered through many lectures by people who don't really care about them. Your validation of their emotions may be a rare gift that they have never received before.

No expression suppression; instead, question. People who don't like you love to talk. People who do like you love to talk. Yes, there are a few who don't want to engage, but they are the minority. You can help a person communicate by asking questions that draw out the healthy parts of them. Those healthy parts may override their incompetent and damaged parts, and you may find yourself with a growing and better relationship.

Don't escalate; deactivate. Stay calm and don't react; most likely, that calmness will rub off on the other person. It is easy to make things worse, but the wise person learns to model peace—and often that is all it takes to make peace.

Key Points to Remember

- Good communication skills are vital for keeping stepfamilies strong.
- Positive communication patterns build connection and intimacy in stepfamilies. These include active listening, open and flexible communication, using constructive conflict management skills, offering praise, expressing empathy, and other nonintrusive caring behaviors.
- Parents and stepparents need to be direct and as open as possible with their children and stepchildren when communicating by being transparent, authentic, and honest about how they feel.

- We can improve communication with our children by helping them deal with their feelings, engaging their cooperation, encouraging autonomy, using praise and self-esteem words, avoiding dead-end questions, and seeking apology and repair when we have done wrong.
- Communication styles that have a tendency to alienate people can be anger, conflict avoidance and stonewalling, mixed messages, passive-aggressive behavior, criticism, contempt, and defensiveness.
- Healthy communication with the other parent can be hard sometimes because there are still intense emotions of jealousy, anger, or sadness coming from both directions. Restricting conversations to only topics concerning the children's welfare is important.

CHAPTER 8

Interpersonal Skills
for Stepfamilies

One morning before school, fifteen-year-old Isabella came into the kitchen while tugging on her shirt. "What do you think about this shirt?" she asked.

Her stepmother, Natalia, held back the words she really wanted to say. "Hmmm, sounds like you don't like it," she said instead. "What's the matter?"

"Oh, I'm not sure," Isabella muttered. "I think it's too tight and I'm not sure about the color." She went on talking about the material, how long it was, and the shape. Then she smiled and said, "Oh well, I'm going to wear it anyway."

Natalia couldn't believe her ears. Isabella didn't want her opinion. All she wanted was a listener. Her counselor had given her sound advice on becoming a better listener. For kids' minor concerns, all she needed to do was show attention by saying "hmmm," or "oh really," followed by a few words of summary. Natalia smiled to herself as she realized Isabella had solved her own concern without her input.

Research over the years has shown that successful stepfamilies have more effective interpersonal skills than those that struggle.[1] Strong interpersonal skills are an asset that can help stepfamilies navigate challenges, adjustments, and day-to-day tasks. So what exactly are interpersonal skills? They are the behaviors one relies on to interact with and communicate with others. Fundamentally, interpersonal skills are about building relationships with others.

Interpersonal skills give stepfamilies indispensable tools for creating a rich and caring environment in which children can find the support they need to learn, grow, and flourish. This chapter will discuss some of the interpersonal skills everyone in the family needs to reduce conflict and defuse charged situations.

Communication Skills

Good communication skills are essential to having a peaceful and loving stepfamily. University of California-Santa Barbara Professor Tamara Afifi says, "Communication is vital to the creation and maintenance of a strong stepfamily."[2] Biological and bonus parents can help their kids learn and practice these important skills.

Previously we looked at active listening skills as they relate to conflict management in the stepfamily. Listening is also a form of connecting more intimately with others. Make yours count by really listening to what your children are saying without adding your opinion or judgment.

- Stop what you are doing and turn to look at the other person. Listen with your ears, eyes, and heart to understand what the person is saying. Listen to their feelings and think about putting yourself in their place.

- Repeat in your own words what they said as a way to let them know you were listening and that you understood. Ask polite questions if you need to understand more of what they said.

- Accept and respect the other person's feelings or point of view, even if you disagree, by saying something like, "I can see why your stepbrother coming into your room without asking would make you angry." Simply listening and not adding your opinion or judgment is vital to the person feeling heard.

Use "I" statements to communicate feelings and desired behaviors. Just as using "I" statements helps the listener not to feel attacked, it also helps you state what you are feeling and what specific behaviors you would like to see changed.

- Say what you are feeling and what you need and want in a respectful way.
- Be specific about what you want and what behavior is bothering you without blaming the other person.
- Avoid "you" statements. For example, avoid statements like, "You are so inconsiderate when you…"

It's wonderful when a family discusses things and the members feel heard, respected, and valued. However, there are communication blockers that can raise walls in listeners. Sarcasm, name-calling, swearing, defensiveness, or refusing to admit there is a problem are all examples of communication blockers. Avoid these with great care.

Improving Concentration

This may not seem like an interpersonal skill, but learning to improve concentration or mental focus helps children control their impulses, stay on task, and deal with emotions. These are all part of interacting with others. This skill helps children learn to pay attention to what is going on at the present time.

One of the ways to increase your ability to stay focused is to be aware of daily activities you are already doing but don't usually give much thought to. Think of daily activities during which you could focus, such as brushing your teeth, taking a shower, getting dressed, brushing your hair, or doing a chore. Take a deep, slow breath as you begin your activity. Intently focus on each part of it. Notice all the details that you usually don't pay attention to. For example, as you are getting dressed, notice the colors of your clothes and how it feels when the material touches different parts of your body. Notice how the clothes feel as you walk around after getting dressed. If you get distracted by thoughts or something else, bring your focus back to the activity.

Some children have problems with following directions. Encourage them to develop this skill by looking at the person when they are speaking to them; repeating the instructions back and saying "okay"; doing the best they can with what has been asked; and if appropriate, reporting back to the person who gave them the instructions when finished. Here's an example: "Don't forget to park your bike in the garage, pick up the toys on the driveway, and close the garage door. Would you please repeat that to me?" Repeating what was said will help them hear the directions again, and it encourages the skills of speaking and listening.

Friendship Skills

Friendship is one of life's greatest gifts. The social skill of getting along with others is an important asset for children to learn as they grow to be healthy and responsible adults. This skill often starts in the family, but it can also apply to people outside the home at school, church, and in the neighborhood. As parents and stepparents, we can set our children up for success by helping them learn how to make friends, keep friends, handle peer pressure, and resolve conflicts peacefully.

Handling Anger

Anger is a natural emotion, but we still need skills to deal with it. Whether it comes from us or is directed at us, anger can cause problems in communication and, if not dealt with properly, damage relationships.

John Gottman has stated that self-regulation, the ability to bring ourselves back into a state of calmness, is the most important interpersonal skill.[3] Self-regulation is about controlling our emotions when we are upset or angry. As your child or stepchild learns how to handle anger, the goal is to be aware of their feelings when they interact with other people. They will then be able to control those feelings while they listen, talk, and act responsibly. This skill will help them get along with others as well as give them confidence in controlling their emotions.

Use the letters *ABCDE* as a fast and easy way to remember how to handle your anger.

A = Aware. Be aware of how your body is reacting so you can notice any clues that you may be getting angry.

B = Breathe. Take a deep breath to help calm yourself.

C = Calm. Think calm and cool thoughts.

D = Defuse. Try to tamp the situation down by calmly asking questions to clarify what the person is saying. Then summarize what you heard them say, even if you don't agree.

E = Escape. Take a break if you start to feel overwhelmed or the other person is too angry. You could say something like, "Let me get back with you after I've had some time to think about what we've discussed."

Handling Negative Consequences

It's never fun when your child or stepchild gets a negative consequence for disobeying rules or hurting others or things. However, the negative consequence lets them know when they've made a wrong choice and need to change their behavior so they can have a happier life by doing what they are supposed to do. For example, "You know the rules. If you miss the bus in the morning, you have to start going to bed thirty minutes earlier to help you not be tired so you will get up on time."

Staying calm is important for your child when he gets a negative consequence because it will show he is able to control himself, too. And when he has more self-control, there will be fewer consequences. Here are some additional tips to go over with your children when they get a negative consequence:

- Stay calm because it can keep the consequence from getting worse.
- Admit and accept the responsibility for your wrongdoing. This is part of being mature.
- Take a slow, deep breath through your nose and let it out through your mouth to help yourself relax.
- Apologize sincerely when you make a mistake.

Understanding Aggressive, Passive, and Assertive Statements

One of my favorite exercises I use in my adolescent anger management classes is to identify the differences between aggressive, passive, and assertive communication and behavior. One way I explain it is: aggressive says, "I count, you don't"; passive says, "You count, I don't"; and assertive says, "I count, but so do you." Being aggressive is being concerned only for yourself and trying to get your way by being threatening. Passive is allowing others to dominate you because of fear and lack of self-respect. Being assertive is being respectful toward yourself, the other person, and your relationship.

Some of the teens in my classes have shared that they think they have to act angry or aggressive to get what they want. This is not true. When we use assertiveness to say what we need and want, it helps people respect us and helps the relationship.

Here are examples comparing aggressive, passive, and assertive statements:

Scenario #1

Aggressive: "Shut up already on the humming. You are such a brat when I'm trying to watch TV."

Passive: Saying to yourself, "I guess it's okay for my sister to hum while I'm watching TV. If I say something, it will start a fight. Whatever!"

Assertive: "I feel annoyed when you hum while I am watching TV. Can you please stop or go somewhere else to hum?"

Scenario #2

Aggressive: "Give me back my CD," as the brother shoves his stepsister. "If you go into my room again to borrow my things without asking, you're going to be sorry!"

Passive: "Whatever, it doesn't matter what she does, she never gets in trouble anyway."

Assertive: "It's not okay with me when you go into my room and borrow my things. I want you to ask first. Please hand over my CD."

Reducing Stress Skills

Stress is a problem for everyone, not just adults. For some children and teenagers, there is stress about school, sports, and homework. That's not counting the pressures that go along with being in a stepfamily. That's a lot for kids to have on their minds. When children don't know how to handle stress, they feel like their world is falling apart. Here are some skills for kids to master in dealing with stress.

Challenge negative self-talk

It's worth mentioning again the importance of helping children recognize and challenge their negative thinking. I feel so strongly about this skill that I teach every child and teenager I see in counseling to be proficient at it. The world is always telling our children they are not enough and must be a certain way to be accepted. I believe if more children mastered this skill, there would be less insecurity, jealousy, self-loathing, and maybe a little less conflict in the world. And who wouldn't want their children to be confident, have good self-esteem, and be easier to get along with?

Breathe calmly

I've mentioned breathing exercises several times throughout this book because they are perhaps one of the best and easiest ways to deal with stress. Teach your child this breathing skill: take a deep breath for a count of six, hold the breath for a count of four, and then release the breath over a count of six. Repeat this several times until your child begins to feel calmer and more alert.

Prioritize physical activity

Samantha comes home from youth group upset. Some of the kids purposefully left her out of an invitation to a swim party. "Mom, I hate them all. It's a stupid youth group anyway." Mom suggests, "Let's go for a walk outside and talk about what happened." Any kind of physical activity that gets your kid's body moving is a way to get the stress out. And it's a great distraction. You can also encourage your child to ask a family member to play a game, build something, or play with the family pet.

Imagine the warm waterfall

This stress-relieving exercise is known as progressive muscle relaxation, but for children I use the words "warm waterfall." Have your child close her eyes and tense all her muscles. Then have her imagine a slow, warm waterfall pouring over her head, down her face, and all the way down to her toes. As the warm water touches each part, relax that set of muscles. Then at the end, have her open her eyes and step out of the make-believe "puddle," completely relaxed and calm.

Modeling Interpersonal Skills

Children and stepchildren learn a great deal about how to act by watching the adults in their lives. Help the young people in your life by modeling healthy and positive inter-personal skills. Let them see how important it is to relax, treat others with respect, and do what is right.

Values influence the way we see the world, the decisions we make, and ultimately our behavior itself. Values help us know who we are and what we stand for. They are the family's personal beliefs about what is important and what is not. Here are just a few examples of family values.

Having a relationship with God

A life centered on God brings stability and strength. Being aware of God helps us acknowledge that life is bigger than we are. Teach your children this value by taking them to church, praying with them, reading and discussing the Bible together, and describing for them what your relationship with God looks like.

Being honest

Let children see you answer questions honestly. Show them it's important to not leave out details to misrepresent what happened. Part of honesty is admitting to mistakes and offering to make amends.

Having courage

Recognizing that our fears can be caused by our thoughts is a form of courage. Keeping our self-talk positive is important, as is replacing negative self-talk with the truth. Speaking up respectfully when one sees a wrong being done is also a form of courage.

Showing kindness

There is no greater value to teach our children than the importance of kindness. I once had a patient say kindness was genetic. But it is not hereditary. It is learned. It's important for us to teach our children to be kind to themselves, as they can be very hard on themselves when things are challenging. As parents, we need to be kind to our children and stepchildren to show them they are deeply loved and valuable.

Respecting others

Teach your children to respect others by using kind and respectful words as you interact with them. Give them your full attention when they are talking to you. Seek to understand what is going on by listening to their feelings and what they need. Parents can help children label their feelings. Control your emotions during difficult interactions with your children as well as with others to show your children what it looks like to be self-controlled.

Teamwork

The value of teamwork keeps our children from becoming entitled and self-absorbed. We need to help them understand the value of teamwork by giving them chores and responsibilities in the home. Family is the first team we belong to. Being part of a team through a club or sporting event can also show them the importance of supportive and successful relationships.

Modeling Healthy Stress Management

Think about how you handle stress. Your children probably handle stress based on how they've seen you handle it. Keep yourself healthy by exercising regularly, eating healthy foods, getting enough sleep, and taking time each day to unwind. Model healthy stress management to your kids by using humor. Show them how to not cram their schedules full so they are not overwhelmed. Treat yourself to a warm bath or listen to music that relaxes you. Through your modeling, your children will see how important it is to know how to relax and de-stress.

Closing Thoughts from Steve

Here is an overused saying that is more true than trite: "More is caught than taught." The kids are watching us, and our actions are screaming at them much louder than our words. The older our kids are, the less teaching and dictating we are doing and the more consulting we provide.

Dictators produce angry and rebellious children. Detached parents fail at providing a model for redemptive relationships. Ask yourself what your children are seeing rather than what you are teaching. It could be the beginning of you making needed changes to become the parent that models compassion, love, and godly character.

Key Points to Remember

- Successful stepfamilies have more effective interpersonal skills than struggling ones.
- Communication is vital to the creation and maintenance of a strong stepfamily.
- The interpersonal skill of getting along with others is an important asset for children to have in order to become healthy and responsible adults.

- Learning to improve concentration or mental focus helps children control their impulses, stay on task, and deal with emotions.
- Children learn valuable social skills through friendships that will benefit them throughout their lives.
- Anger-management skills help children get along with others and give them confidence in controlling their emotions.
- Parents can encourage stress-management skills in their children by teaching them techniques such as challenging negative thoughts, deep breathing, and progressive relaxation.
- Children learn a great deal about how to act by watching the adults in their lives.

CHAPTER 9

Understanding Your Bonus Child's Personality

The HGTV program *House Hunters* is one of my favorites to watch. My love for beautiful houses started when I was a child, when my grandparents would pile our family in their large car on Sunday afternoons and drive us around the neighborhoods to look at homes my grandmother, an interior decorator, had recently finished. We couldn't see into the homes she had decorated, but she would describe each beautiful room in detail.

Stepfamilies are like beautiful homes we can see only from the outside. However, there is a lot more going on inside. Each beautiful stepfamily has members with different personalities, just as a home has differently decorated rooms. Because members of stepfamilies live under the same roof, it's vital for them to get to know each other's likes, dislikes, strengths, and weaknesses in order to live together effectively, just as it's important for new homeowners to know the function of each room in their house.

Who Are You, and Who Is Your Bonus Child?

When children are born, they usually grow up with their family and get to know each member by seeing his or her strengths and weaknesses over time. But in stepfamilies, children haven't had the chance to get to know each other through the years. They are instantly living together under the same roof without an intimate knowledge of each member. This is why when a blended family comes in to me for counseling, the first things we talk about are the members' strengths, weaknesses, and love languages.

During my doctoral program, I studied many personality assessments created to help people see their own strengths and weaknesses. However, even though these assessments were informative, they were very long, and the results were complicated. For a quick and simple tool to understand stepfamily members' personalities, I recommend these resources: the personality tool from *Personality Plus* by Florence Littauer,[1] *The 5 Love Languages of Children* by Gary Chapman,[2] and *How We Love* by Milan and Kay Yerkovich.[3] I encourage stepfamilies to have these books on hand as a reference guide while they continue to adjust to each other.

The books include questionnaires, charts, and ideas on how to get to know your own personality as well as your children's. The *Personality Plus* tool can be found at several online sites. Chapman's questionnaires are free at https://www.5lovelanguages.com/quizzes, and the Yerkoviches have a free quiz at https://howwelove.com/love-style-quiz. It's important for adults not only to understand their children's personalities, but to understand their own as well and how they impact stepfamily dynamics.

A crucial part of understanding and loving your bonus children is understanding how they receive love. According to Chapman, "Children receive love emotionally. But because they are all different, we must pay attention to their individual needs. We must learn to speak our children's [love] language if we want them to feel loved."[4] Here are the five love languages as described in the book:

- **Affirming words:** words of affection, endearment, praise, and encouragement
- **Quality time:** focused, undivided attention; being together
- **Gifts:** giving and receiving of unexpected gifts

- **Acts of service:** services for your children that *they* see as valuable
- **Physical touch:** hugs, cuddles, kisses, and pats on the back

When your child feels loved, he is much easier to guide and discipline than when his "emotional tank" is running near empty. According to Chapman, by speaking your child's love language, you can fill his "emotional tank" with love that he best understands.

Here are some ideas to get you started.

Affirming words

- Compliment and praise your children for specific things. For example, "Thank you for helping me!" or "You did really well at that!"
- Write encouraging notes for them to find around the house or to put in their lunch boxes.
- Say positive things about them to others and let them overhear.

Quality time

- Talk together one-on-one.
- Practice sports or a hobby together.

- Do homework or chores together.
- Give undivided attention: read a story together; kick a ball outside.
- Take a trip to the cinema or go to a special place for a snack together.

Unexpected gifts

- Leave a surprise treat in their bag or under their pillow.
- Give them a small gift after a particularly challenging time.
- Mail them small gifts when you are away.
- Make sure you express your love verbally or in writing with the gift.

Acts of service

- Help them with a school project.
- Make their favorite meal or snack as a surprise.
- Take them someplace they enjoy.

Physical touch

- Give them frequent hugs, pats on the back, high fives, and cuddles.

- Sit together in a chair or bean bag to watch TV or read a book.
- Incorporate physical activities like racing, wrestling, playing tag, and climbing into your lap.

If you are still struggling to identify your child's love language, here are a few things that may give clues:

- How your child expresses love to you
- How your child expresses love to others
- Listen to what your child requests most often
- Notice what your child most frequently complains about
- Give your child a choice between two options, and see what they most frequently choose

One stepparent I saw in counseling decided to simply ask the children, "How do you know your daddy or mommy love you?" Six-year-old Samantha replied, "Mommy hugs me and kisses me before I go anywhere and before I go to bed at night." Her answer suggests hers may be the love language of physical touch. Twelve-year-old Henry shared, "Dad buys me cool rockets, and we build them together and shoot them off at the park." He has both gifts and quality time as his love languages.

Discovering your child's love language will depend partly on his or her age. Babies, toddlers, and preschoolers don't yet have a primary love language and need to be shown love in lots of different ways. Kids aged five to twelve will likely tell you what theirs is if you ask. Teenagers are harder to reach. You could try emailing them the "Discover Your Love Language" quiz from Chapman's website and invite them to chat afterward about the results. Or you could think back on how your teenager normally lets you know they love their biological parent. Perhaps they offer hugs, buy thoughtful gifts for their friends, or do a chore without being asked. They are most likely to express love in the way they like to receive it.

In Chapman's book *Building Love Together in Blended Families*, coauthored with Ron Deal, he reminds readers to keep in mind that:

> It's very different because the family has been put together without everyone's consent, mainly the children. Often times, blended families are not as motivated by love as the biological family. In blended families, there can be an attitude of not caring about receiving or giving love to the people who are not their family. And of course the family dynamics are very different in the blended family.[5]

In the book *How We Love*, the Yerkoviches present a quick tool that dives more into the psychological approach of understanding how we attach and bond with others. It helps parents identify their own childhood wounds that may create triggers in the present, which in turn impact how they love and parent their kids. The Yerkoviches explain how each person's childhood experiences form the roots of who they are, continuing to inform the way that person responds to others or expresses love, even far into adulthood. The results of all these experiences are actually predictable because people tend to fall into one of five special categories, called "love styles."[6]

Once you determine your love style, the Yerkoviches provide information about each style and how it responds to stress, triggers, goals, expectations, feelings, and needs. The assessment also helps you look at your love style and how it interacts with other people's. The tools I've discussed will all help stepparents understand their bonus children to a greater degree. Their methods differ: *Personality Plus* helps you understand your child's personality traits, strengths, and weaknesses; *The 5 Love Languages* shows how your child receives love; and *How We Love* helps parents understand how they attach and bond with others. All give stepparents and biological parents tools to help the relationships in their stepfamilies run more smoothly. But keep in mind to go slowly and take small steps with the information you learn. Take your time when getting to know your bonus child. It's a marathon, not a sprint.

Bonus children may not be as excited as you are about the new information you've discovered about your personality and theirs. Many stepparents have asked me, "What happens if my stepchild doesn't like me or we can't get along?" I gently encourage them that it's okay, and they can still work on developing respect in the relationship. Love does not happen overnight. It doesn't mean stepparents have failed when their stepchild doesn't warm up to them. It just takes time. Start with small things like walking the dog together or asking your stepchild to help you with a project before you tackle major issues like behaviors. And when misunderstandings inevitably occur, talk through them calmly and respectfully. Keep in mind that you're all in the same family and on the same side.

Choosing to stay the course and not give up when things don't go as planned is important. We become great stepparents by learning about our children's personality and learning what they need. I remind stepparents having a difficult time integrating as a family to think back to the beginning and remember why they came together in the first place. Every relationship has its own set of challenges, but love is the foundation.

Closing Thoughts from Steve

"Acceptance is the answer to all my problems today." This is my favorite quote of all time; it comes from the "Big Book" of *Alcoholics Anonymous* by Bill Wilson. I have tried to disprove it, but it applies to everything—including bonus children. Each one is different, and each one comes with varying levels of difficulty. Sometimes it is easy to accept them, and often it is not. We need to work on loving and accepting each one. That means discovering why it is not easy. If the reason is that their unique personality triggers something unhealthy or painful in you, go to work on that unresolved issue so you can be the bonus parent your bonus child needs.

Key Points to Remember

- Stepfamilies haven't had the chance to get to know each other through the years like biological families do.
- Each stepfamily has members with different personalities, just as a home is made up of different rooms.
- Learn about your personality as well as your bonus child's to help the family adjust more smoothly.

- Use the assessments in *Personality Plus, How We Love*, and *The 5 Love Languages* to understand your bonus child's personality and your own.
- Go slowly and take small steps as family members adjust to each other.
- Be patient when getting to know your bonus child. It is a marathon, not a sprint.

CHAPTER 10

Increasing Happiness in Stepchildren

All parents want their children to be happy. However, with the complications of divorce, remarriages, and adjustments to new stepfamilies, *happy* is not usually the first word stepparents would use to describe their bonus kids. Even though stepfamilies have their own unique set of challenges, it's good to remember that happiness is a learned skill. Parents and stepparents can teach their children and stepchildren to be happy; this skill can have a tremendous impact on their children's outlook on life. Psychologist Barbara Fredrickson found happy children are more likely to become successful adults who do well at work and love. In addition, they usually are healthier and may even live longer![1]

This chapter will address how parents and stepparents can teach their children to have a happy childhood in spite of their circumstances. The happiness skills in this chapter will include gratitude, kindness, self-discipline, understanding emotions, happiness habits, optimism, faith, confidence, and connection to others.

Boost Your Own Happiness

I realize this chapter is about teaching your children to be happy, but one of the best things you can do for your children is to work on being happy yourself. It's a lot harder to teach your children how to be happy when you are unhappy. Happy parents are great role models.

Research shows that children will imitate their parents' emotions.[2] So if you are finding the good in situations, or being kind to a neighbor, your children are likely to follow in your footsteps and do the same. If you're not happy, it's never too late to get happier. There are many ways to increase your happiness as an adult:

- Spend time with friends who make you laugh; laughter releases endorphins, the chemicals that make us feel good.

- Get massages from your partner, your kids, or at a spa. Getting a massage not only makes us feel relaxed, calm, and content due to chemical changes in our brain, but it also reduces stress hormones.
- Get outdoors, since nature increases positive emotions. Take a walk, ride your bike on a trail, or take nature photographs.
- Implement relaxation into your life by having some personal quiet time, whether it's outdoors or at your favorite quiet place in your home. This shows your children the importance of quietness and self-care.
- Prioritize your relationship with your partner by making time to communicate, handle conflict positively, and show respect, admiration, affection, and attentiveness.

Teach Them Faith

When I was growing up, my parents constantly modeled their faith at home as well as in the community. Little did I know as a child that their faith in God would be the best tradition they would pass down to me. Faith taught me how to love and care for people, how to do what is right, and the importance of having a personal relationship with Jesus Christ. This heritage has helped me deal with the struggles as well as the joys in life. Faith that we pass down to our children will help guide them when they feel alone or when things seem hopeless.

It's never too late to start. Find a Bible-based church in your area that emphasizes the Scripture as God's truth, and take your family to church. Start reading Bible stories with them or have them read the stories out loud during family time or before bed. Teach them to pray so they know God is there 24/7. Share how God has helped you through struggles, and praise Him for His faithfulness.

Family Dinners

When I think of my family dinners growing up, I think of prayer, food, and conversations that happened around our table. Family dinners are powerful. Recent research shows that children who enjoy family meals have larger vocabularies, better manners, healthier diets, and higher self-esteem.[3] Use family dinners as a time to share family history. Encourage the children to talk so they can learn how to have conversations with others, but also teach them to listen to the adults so they can learn how to interact and speak correctly. Pick a variety of topics to talk about. One family shared in counseling that they make conversation fun by putting questions inside a jar so family members can draw one out. For example, "What is the funniest thing that's ever happened to you?" or "What traits do you look for in a friend?"

If your schedules are busy, shoot for family dinner once a week, as it still makes a difference. And it doesn't have to be dinner. It can be breakfast on Saturday mornings or a picnic lunch outside or inside. The important thing is to do it on a regular basis.

Encourage Relationships and Kindness

Connections with other people are important to our children's happiness. It's important for parents to have relationships too. We all need community. As parents, we can encourage family ties with "surrogate parents," such as grandparents, aunts, uncles, neighbors, or people who attend church with us. Teach your children how to get along with others and how to resolve conflicts peacefully. This skill will come in handy not only with their friends now, but will help them be successful as adults when they are dealing with people at work or in the community.

It's important to note here that you don't have to be biologically related to a child to make an impact in his or her life.

As I've worked with people in counseling over the years, I've heard time and again how a stepparent or other caring adult made a difference in someone's life because they took the time to listen and make themselves reliably available to the child.

Part of being in relationships is being kind. People are not naturally born with kindness, but it can be learned with practice. Parents can model kindness and empathy to their children by comforting and consoling them when they are hurting. When you see a two-year-old comforting another child who is upset, it is because they have had kindness and empathy modeled for them. Parents' kindness and empathy sets a foundation for the child to work from as they help others. Let your child see you helping others by taking meals to someone sick or volunteering in the community at a nonprofit organization.

Here are additional ideas to foster kindness in your children:

- Praise your children verbally when they are showing kindness to others, such as, "That was very nice of you to share half of your cookie with the boy on the playground," or "How thoughtful of you to take the neighbor's dog for a walk while she is recuperating from surgery."

- Encourage them to do small acts of kindness such as baking cookies for a sick neighbor, holding the door for someone who has their hands full, or visiting a nursing home.
- Set up opportunities for them to help others by volunteering where there is a need, such as pet rescues, helping an elderly neighbor with gardening, or helping out at church programs during the summer.
- Verbally acknowledge the facial and bodily expressions of other people when they are hurting so children can see and feel things from another person's perspective. For example, "It's not nice that people are laughing at the waitress who spilled tea down the front of her shirt. She looks sad and embarrassed."
- Provide books for your children that encourage kindness and compassion.

Avoid Coddling

The definition of coddling, according to *Macmillan Dictionary*, is "to treat someone in a way that gives them too much protection from harm or difficult experiences."[4] Parents have a natural desire to protect their babies, and they need to take care of their infants' immediate needs. When those needs are met, it shows the infants that they have a safe environment and can trust those caring for them. However, coddling becomes an issue as the children get older.

Bonnie Harris, founder of Core Parenting and author of *When Your Kids Push Your Buttons: And What You Can Do About It*, states, "If we put our kids in a bubble and grant them their every wish and desire, that is what they grow to expect, but the real world doesn't work that way."[5] Sometimes parents have a hard time allowing their children to experience disappointments and frustrations. They want to immediately run to their children's sides and get rid of anything causing them unhappiness. Harris warns that if children never learn to deal with negative emotions, they will be in danger of being crushed by them as adolescents and adults.

Instead of coddling your children and adolescents by doing everything for them, bring them up to be independent and emotionally healthy people who can solve problems and conflicts on their own. This will help them learn that life can sometimes be unfair, and they will not always get their way. Coddling sets them up for failure later in life. All that said, it can definitely be a balancing act—trying to find the right amount of guidance while letting the child build his self-esteem by making his own decisions.

Coddling can happen in every family, stepfamilies included. Divorces can sometimes make the adults feel guilty about what their children have gone through. If adults feel guilty about not spending enough time with their children, this can cause them to coddle as a way to make up for lost time or overindulge the children with anything that will make them happy. This only sets the child up for failure in life. Parents must find that balancing act of providing guidance and yet not stepping in at every moment so the child can learn how to handle different situations. Naturally, it's wise to take into account the child's age, maturity level, and circumstances.

Rules and Discipline

This is always a difficult topic. Rather than being oppressive, rules can be things children can count on. Keep in mind that their whole world has been turned upside down, and they need stability. In a household with inconsistent or nonexistent rules, children experience uncertainty. Kids want an environment where they know what is going to happen next and what is expected of them. Believe it or not, they want boundaries and want to know what the rules are. Obviously, they are not going to come to you asking for rules, but they do get a sense of security knowing there are rules in place.

Work as a team with your spouse. Don't worry about what other blended families are doing as far as rules and discipline. Stay focused on your home. Be consistent with the rules and boundaries. This will help your children become adults who are successful in the world.

Assign Real Responsibilities

I believe in chores for the entire family. As parents (stepparents included), part of our job is to help our kids became successful adults. Chores help kids become more responsible. A chore routine gives them structure and helps them know how to do things when they move out on their own.

According to Julie Lythcott-Haims, author of the *New York Times* bestseller *How to Raise an Adult*, it's important for children to help around the house with chores. In her research, she found people generally need two things to be successful in life. The first is love, and the second is a work ethic.[6] Children develop a work ethic by having chores like washing dishes, taking care of pets, cleaning their rooms, helping with dinner, taking out the garbage, etc. It may seem easier to do it ourselves, but it isn't teaching them the work ethic that will make them productive, successful adults. They will realize that part of life is doing work—like chores.

Parents have shared with me two schools of thought on chores and responsibilities for their children. One side says let children be children and have fun without chores since their entire adult lives will be full of responsibilities. The other side says that children need chores to learn skills to handle their adult lives. I believe there needs to be a balance of fun and responsibilities as children grow up. I wholeheartedly believe children and adolescents learn many skills by having chores and responsibilities at home. Part of happiness is feeling that what we do matters and is of value to others. All children need to feel they are making a contribution and are part of the family team. When they are acknowledged for making a contribution to the family, their sense of belonging and confidence increases.

Start by having your children help with household chores at an early age. Sometimes parents think it would be easier if they went ahead and did the chore themselves. You could do it faster and probably with less effort than trying to teach your child how to do it, but your child would get the message that chores are for adults only. If you teach them early, they can progress naturally to accepting more and more responsibilities, until one day they may be doing chores better than you!

There are plenty more reasons for assigning chores to all children.

New skills

Children will gain skills they will need later in life. They will eventually have a home that needs to be cleaned and organized; chores teach them how to do this under their parents' guidance.

Being a team player

Being part of a family teaches children how to listen, compromise, ask for help, and be a committed team player by completing responsibilities that benefit the whole family.

Time management

Chores help children figure out how long something may take. As they get older, allow them to be part of the process of deciding when and how the chores will be done. This will give them more confidence and foster the skill of learning to plan their time wisely.

Self-sufficiency

When children know they can accomplish chores on their own, they gain a sense of self-worth and independence.

Sense of accomplishment

Nothing feels better than stepping back and reviewing your hard work on a chore that looks great. Plus, it feels good to be able to contribute something to the family team and not just be a benchwarmer. Parents can add to this feeling by complimenting and acknowledging the completed chore.

I want to add a very important note. Although chores are part of helping our kids become responsible adults, there are days that schedules are crazy busy. Sometimes the chore chart may not get followed exactly. There may be nights when sports or other activities take kids out of town, and they don't get home until very late. But having a chore chart up in a central location creates a visual reminder of what has to be done. The kids can check the chart on the days they are not so busy and still do the chores they were not able to do when they got home late. Flexibility with chores is important.

Don't Forget Playtime

Children play in order to learn. Playing creates a place for them to learn emotional, social, and physical skills such as self-regulating, working with others, sharing, resolving conflicts, and speaking up for themselves. In the book *Play: How It Shapes the Brain, Opens the Imagination, and Invigorates the Soul*, Stuart Brown states that playfulness is associated with better academic performance due to the brain learning to stay more focused while learning.[7] In other words, students who are more playful do better in school. Playtime is not just goofing off. It's very important in helping kids grow and learn.

Praise Effectively

Parents want to make their children feel good and happy, but sometimes they can become overzealous and praise their children for every little thing. The problem with this is that the child will begin to think the only way to get parental approval is through doing something for praise. Instead of praising the result or achievement, praise the effort. Bob Murray suggests in his book *Raising an Optimistic Child* to "Praise the creativity, the hard work, the persistence, that goes into achieving, more than the achievement itself."[8] An example would be simple praise, such as, "You must have worked very hard on that puzzle," or "You did well on cleaning your room." Additional ideas on how to praise your children are:

Don't overdo it

It's good to make a big deal about a major achievement, like the first time your toddler picks up his toys or your teenager passes a major test he studied hard for. But going overboard on every little daily achievement like, "Yay, you let the dog out!" or "Wow, you brushed your teeth!" will only cheapen praise for something he's truly earned.

Avoid bragging

When you brag in public about your child, it not only annoys other parents, but it puts a lot of pressure on the child to perform and get your approval.

Be honest

Children can see right through fake compliments. The best thing to do is be honest. If your child keeps falling down when learning to skate, don't say, "Wow, you're doing great!" Instead, a better way to praise is, "You are working hard at trying to skate." This way the child knows you are being truthful and yet praising their efforts.

Be specific

When you are praising a behavior, focus on specifics so the child understands exactly what you are praising. For example, instead of saying, "You were great in the grocery store today," be specific and say, "You were quiet and stayed right beside the shopping cart." This allows the child to understand what behavior earns him a compliment.

Teach Optimism and Gratitude

To put it simply, optimism is being able to look on the bright side of situations. According to author Christine Carter, optimism is so closely related to happiness that the two can practically be the same.[9] Compared to pessimistic people, optimists are more successful at school, work, and athletics; they are healthier and live longer; they are more satisfied with their marriages; and they are less likely to deal with depression and anxiety. Here are a few ideas on how children can learn to be optimistic.

Allow risks and failure

Children need to be able to cope with difficulties and frustration in order to develop optimism. Parents need to allow children to make mistakes so they can learn from them. As Carter points out, this also teaches children how to overcome challenges in the future and makes them feel hopeful.

Model optimism

Don't just model optimism for your children, but model how to interpret events that happen in your life. Children are watching the adults in their lives and mimic their mindsets and reactions. Teach your children to identify the good that comes out of difficulties or think about what they can learn from failure. When you hear them make pessimistic statements, help them turn the statement around by choosing a more optimistic thought.

Feelings of gratitude are part of being happy. Children who practice grateful thinking have more positive attitudes toward school and their parents.[10] As parents we can encourage gratitude by making it a family ritual to ask our children daily at dinner or bedtime to say aloud what they are thankful for. Older children can keep a journal of things they are thankful for and share those with their families. Parents can share their gratitude lists as well as a way to model this positive exercise.

Encourage Self-Discipline Skills

The ability to self-discipline (or self-regulate, as scientists call it) is an important key to success and happiness. Self-disciplined children cope better with frustration and stress and have more social responsibility. They also do better in school, have more friends, and are more involved in the community.[11] The following are some techniques Carter recommends to help children build self-regulation skills.

Reduce their stress

If a child is worried about his parents fighting, school grades, or anything stressful in his environment, he will find it harder to have self-control.

Turn off the TV

Television or any kind of screen time in itself is not evil, but it does take up time that the children could be playing and using their imaginations and social skills. The television and computer do not increase their willpower or help with impulse control.

Self-discipline games

Play games with your kids that teach self-regulation, such as Simon Says or freeze tag. These encourage children to have to think in order to not do something. Cooking and following a recipe with directions is also a great way for them to delay gratification because they have to go through steps in order to make something.

Help them develop self-discipline through distraction

Parents can help children find ways to distract themselves when they are tempted by something in their environment. For example, give the child a toy to play with or ask her to think about something fun. This models to the child the concept of distraction, which they can eventually start doing on their own without the parents prompting. Distraction can be a form of self-discipline which can help children cope better with frustration and stress.

Have realistic expectations

It's unrealistic to think young children under the age of four can have self-control or delay gratification.

Be Their Emotion Coach

As parents, it's important to be loving and engaged with our children. Part of loving them is teaching them how to cope with negative feelings like sadness and disappointment. Research by relationship expert John Gottman shows that emotional awareness and the ability to manage feelings will determine how successful and happy our children are throughout life, even more than their IQ.[12] This is what is called emotional intelligence. Increasing your children's emotional intelligence sets them up for a life of happiness by helping them learn about their own feelings as well as the feelings of others. We are not born with this skill, but it can be learned.

The first thing you can do is recognize a child's negative emotion as an opportunity to connect. Dealing with negative emotions in children can be a great teaching moment of bonding, healing, and growing with your child. Listen empathetically to their feelings and let them know you have heard them. Communicate with kindness to let them know their emotions are very intense at the moment. For example, "I can see you are really mad at me right now because I want you to get out of the pool. Swimming is your favorite thing to do, so I understand why you are mad," or, "How frustrating that your little brother stomped on your toy. I completely get it."

Negative emotions are very normal for young children, and kids usually get better at managing them as they get older. Parents reacting negatively or disregarding their children's feelings will send the message that what they are feeling is unimportant or bad. Children then may begin to think they are bad because they have a "bad feeling."

Help your child verbally label his emotions. First, seek to understand by asking questions and let him know you are there for him when things are tough and overwhelming. Next, help your child put words to his feelings. For example, say things like, "I can tell you are really upset right now" or "It sounds like your friend hurt your feelings." Once children are able to recognize their feelings and put them into words, they gradually become able to regulate themselves without getting overwhelmed.

Set limits while helping your child solve problems. Help her find ways to respond differently the next time something similar happens. Use the situation as a teaching moment. Ask for her help in coming up with other ideas about how she could respond to her struggles. We can gently remind our kids that all emotions are okay, but there are certain behaviors that are not okay. For example, "I know it's frustrating when your sister plays with your toys without asking, but pulling her hair is not acceptable. How could you express your feelings next time without hurting her?"

Closing Thoughts from Steve

The responsible parent is a resourcing parent. Troubled children may be one counselor away from happiness, or at least being happier. That counselor could be yours or theirs. If you are a bit low on the happiness scale, it will be difficult to lead your children to greater happiness. If a child has not been given the benefit of a great coach or counselor, now is the time to find the best resource possible. Don't be the unwilling person that stands in the way of a child getting the help that could increase the happiness level of the entire blended family.

Key Points to Remember

- Happiness is a skill that can be learned.
- One of the best things parents can do for their children's emotional well-being is to nurture their own happiness.
- Faith we pass down to our children will help guide them when they feel alone or when things seem hopeless.
- Having meals together as a family results in children having larger vocabularies, better manners, healthier diets, and higher self-esteem.
- Getting along with others and being kind is a skill that can be learned.
- If parents overprotect their children, give them everything they want, and shield them from disappointments, they are setting them up for failure in life, because the real world doesn't work that way.
- Assigning appropriate chores to children helps them learn new skills, become team players, learn time management, become self-sufficient, and have a sense of accomplishment. Chores help kids

develop a work ethic, which helps them become responsible adults.

- Playtime for children creates a place to learn emotional, social, and physical skills.
- Instead of praising children for the result or achievement, praise them for the effort.
- Children who practice optimism and grateful thinking have more positive attitudes toward school and their parents.
- Self-discipline skills help children do better in school, make new friends, and cope better with stress.
- Emotional awareness and the ability to manage feelings will determine how successful and happy our children are throughout life.

CHAPTER 11

Having Fun as a Stepfamily

LaQuita pinched the bridge of her nose and squeezed her eyes tight as she let out a loud sigh. "My stepkids told their dad that they hate coming to our house because it's no fun," she said. "How are we supposed to have fun when there are after-school activities and chores to do?"

Finding the time to play together as a family is often difficult in our fast-paced world. As LaQuita said, blended families with different schedules and routines barely have time for it. I tried to help her understand that kids will feel happy when they are having fun and will begin to associate happiness with the people they are having fun with. Once they see that fun is also a part of their new family, they will likely be more willing to take part in the family chores and feel more positive about the

179

situation. LaQuita learned to make fun an intentional activity, which in turn helped when it was time to deal with chores.

Fun, chores, routines, and traditions combined can create bonds within families. It may seem impossible to think of a stepfamily bonding, but it can happen. There will be times of stress and perhaps even fear of rejection for step-parents and biological parents alike. However, bonding is important and can be filled with fun. Start with small steps, which can add up to strong, secure relationships. Be patient and don't give up.

In addition to having fun as a family, implement fun in all one-on-one relationships. Each person needs one-on-one time with each other individually. For the biological relationships, that may mean a couple of hours, but with the step-relationships, it may be only a fifteen-minute activity. Each individual relationship in your home is important, so find ways to connect.

Here are some activities that can make bonding fun.

Outdoor Fun for Blended Families

Hiking trails

Almost every town has hiking trails or paths around a neighborhood or city park. Some will allow pets too.

Lake, river, or beach

Most children love being near water. You can swim, walk, have a picnic, fish, collect shells, or have a scavenger hunt.

Team sports

Head outside to enjoy soccer, football, basketball, baseball, cornhole, bocce ball, or any team activity. Be sure to keep in mind that sometimes team sports can lead to stress or competitiveness in kids—and adults. If this happens, try to keep the time short and find other activities that are not as stressful and yet interactive for everyone.

Other outdoor activities

- Garden together
- Fly a kite
- Walk a dog—yours or someone else's
- Visit a water park
- Visit a local playground
- Visit the zoo or local aquarium
- Beautify your driveway or sidewalk with chalk art
- Play hide-and-seek
- Go camping
- Go fishing
- Ride go-carts

- Have a fun water gun fight
- Have a snowball fight
- Build a treehouse
- Tune up a car (for teens, include learning about airing up tires, changing a flat, washing and waxing the car, and maybe even changing the oil)
- Go antiquing or to garage sales to find treasures
- Create bug or leaf collections
- Pick and press wildflowers
- Stargaze

Be intentional and creative in all your outdoor activities. Ask the kids if they have ideas. Sometimes they bring the best ideas to the table, and you're sure to get something they're truly interested in.

Indoor Fun for Blended Families

Staying home doesn't have to be boring. Most kids want to immediately default to watching TV or being on the computer or some kind of electronic device. Set limits for those and offer alternative fun activities that get everyone involved.

Movie night

This is a fun activity, but it can take some time to find a movie everyone likes. A movie that makes everyone laugh provides a great bonding moment. Pop some popcorn and enjoy the time as a family.

Family game night

This can include board games, card games, or video games. Some families keep a schedule or calendar of whose turn it is to decide the game. You can add more fun by having game marathons.

Indoor scavenger hunt

This scavenger hunt can be limited to the house or even the yard with weather permitting. You can work in teams or do it individually. Set a time limit and reward the winning team or person with a prize like a movie theater coupon or night off from chores.

Girls' night / guys' night

Pick a night when the girls stay home and camp out in the backyard to stargaze or catch fireflies, learn a new card game, make a craft to take to a nursing home, shoot some hoops, etc., while the guys go volunteer at a homeless shelter, attend a sporting event, or take a road trip without a plan. Then switch it up the next time with guys staying home and girls going out. Be creative and ask for kids' input.

Friendly competition

Any kind of competition can be fun and will be an instant success. My family has timed events of building things out of marshmallows, popcorn, straws, or gumdrops. Sometimes we have cookie-decorating contests or poster contests. Use your imagination and ask the kids for ideas. Fun events will make everyone laugh, and this helps lighten the mood no matter what has been going on. Laughing together as a family will bond you, and laughter is a great stress reliever for everyone.

Serve together

This can be an indoor or outdoor activity. The great part is that it keeps the focus off you and on others. It can be baking cookies for a sick neighbor, mowing the lawn of an elderly person, making a gift for someone, or walking someone's dog. Some stepfamilies serve food at a community Thanksgiving meal. Check out Random Acts of Kindness at randomactsof-kindness.org for great ideas on how to serve others.

Other indoor activity ideas

- Visit a museum
- Cook as a blended family and ensure everyone is included
- Have a picnic inside the house
- Go to an indoor water park
- Play hide-and-seek
- Do some kind of craft
- Visit an indoor aquarium
- Build a blanket fort
- Read a book together
- Put on a family play or puppet show
- Play dress-up from a movie, book, or Bible story
- Dress up nicely as a family and pretend you are at a fancy restaurant
- Have a tea party
- Go bowling
- Play laser tag at an entertainment center
- Play indoor miniature golf
- Have a dance party

Create New Family Traditions

It's important to create new traditions together. These can help make everyone feel part of the new family. Many of my clients who are in blended families have shared their desire for new traditions when split-custody situations mandate alternating holidays with the other parent. Some of the blended families have created new traditions on holidays like the Fourth of July or Valentine's Day. One blended family celebrates Cinco de Mayo since they live in Texas. They travel to San Antonio, where there is a huge Cinco de Mayo celebration on the River Walk. Another blended family that doesn't get to spend Christmas with their kids makes Christmas cookies and gingerbread houses the weekend before as a new way to celebrate the season. They realized that holidays are special because you are together as a family, not because of a date on the calendar. Here are some other ideas for new traditions.

Easter

Have fun decorating or dyeing Easter eggs as a family. Then hide the decorated eggs for the kids to find, perhaps with a grand prize for the one who finds a special egg. Teenagers can help hide the eggs if they don't want to hunt. A service project for the entire family could be to help stuff and hide Easter eggs for a community or church event.

Birthdays

Be sure to celebrate each child's birthday. I believe birthdays become even more important in blended families. Special birthday celebrations reassure children that they are loved and wanted. It's okay if you don't celebrate on the actual date if scheduling conflicts are unavoidable, but it's always important to celebrate their birthdays. Some blended families let the child pick his favorite meal and the rest of the family helps fix it. Buying inexpensive decorations for his bedroom door or the kitchen will add joy to the birthday child's day.

Christmas

Some blended families alternate Christmas with the other biological parent, but you can create your own new traditions whether you celebrate on December 25 or a weekend or two before. As a family, you can make homemade ornaments and decorate the tree. This is fun, and the ornaments can change year to year. One blended family I know goes to the community Angel Tree and selects several children to shop for together. Part of the fun is letting your child pick out the gifts and wrap them.

The busy Christmas season can be very stressful for everyone, including the kids. When they are going to visit all the extended families from both parents and their new stepparents, it can be exhausting, not to mention confusing. Many kids share with me in counseling how they wish things were more relaxed and fun at Christmas instead of rushing around to all the extended families' homes. Encourage your kids to have fun, and be happy for them. This will help them enjoy the holiday more and share their fun with you. Don't feel threatened by time spent with other family members. Just be with your kids, listen to them, and tell them you are happy for them.

The Kindness Key

If your young kids are struggling to be nice to each other, this is a fun way to teach them to be kind to each other and to recognize kindness in others. Draw a wide eight- to twelve-inch key (you can find patterns on Google or Pinterest) and have one of the kids cut it out and another decorate it. Put a string through a hole at the top with enough slack to be able to fit the key over their heads. Place the key so everyone can see it throughout the day. When someone is noticed for being kind, they get to wear the Kindness Key until the next child is recognized for being kind. Keep track of how many times each child wears the key throughout the day. Adults can participate in catching the kids being kind too! At the end of the day, a reward is given to the child with the most kindness acts. Rewards can be a small bag of candy, a coupon for something like ice cream or a snow cone, etc. This is fun and a beautiful thing to witness as kids are being kind and made aware of others' kindness.

Special-recognition plate

When someone has been recognized for an achievement at school or church, set a special plate at that person's place at dinnertime. Keep a special plate that is only for this occasion. One family had a plate with a family photo on it. Another family had a vivid red plate with a heart in the middle. It doesn't matter what the plate looks like as long as everyone knows it's "the special plate." Sometimes the adults decide who gets the special plate and sometimes one of the kids will share with the adults why a sibling should have the special plate that night at dinner. It's a great exercise in helping kids develop empathy and pride in one another.

Rituals and Routines

It may seem impossible to add new rituals and routines to your busy schedules. However, routines can actually save time and help kids feel connected to their new family. Anything can be made into a ritual, from chores to the drive to school or what you do with family on Friday night.

Before blended families start rituals, I encourage the adults to sit down and discuss their own rituals growing up, and then decide together what they want for their blended family. Rituals can be about how you start the day, reunite after work or school, eat dinner, go to bed, or how you spend the weekends, the holidays, or vacations. The adults can bring their ritual ideas to the entire family, explaining to them the desire for family to have common goals, values, and interests. Below are some examples my patients in blended families have implemented.

- The Thompson family goes out for pizza every Friday night to celebrate being back together as a family. They talk about what each member has experienced since the last time they were together. Afterward, they may walk around a nearby park, or go home to play a board game or watch a movie together.
- The Joneses might invite another blended family over on Saturday night and grill hamburgers while the kids play together outside. After dinner, they may play a game of cornhole in the backyard.
- Every Sunday night the Smiths have a quick meeting to go over the family schedule for the week coming up. There is a schedule board that

everyone can see during the meeting and throughout the week.

Joint custody visitation

It may be part of your blended family ritual to have your
spouses' child or children every other weekend. To help the
children adjust and feel like they are part of the family, it's
important for them to have their own private space if possible. You don't want your bonus children to feel like they
are strangers or guests in your home. If space is limited, be
creative and dedicate personal space for them, such as a
certain dresser or closet for their clothes and belongings.
Also, having their favorite toiletries, food, or favorite toys
or games will help them feel like part of the family instead
of like visitors. One large family I worked with in counseling
had six children between them and did not have the space
for each child to have his or her own bedroom. However,
they did designate certain dresser drawers in the bedrooms
and bathrooms for each child.

Attending church

Going to church as a family can be a meaningful ritual,
even though it can be a struggle to get the family up and out
the door on Sunday morning. My family always struggled in

this area; I'm not sure if it was because we were tired from the jam-packed week of activities or if we just were not morning people. One thing I suggest to my clients is trying to go to church on Saturday or Sunday night instead. If possible, try to find a few weekday activities to let go of so the family feels more like going to church on Sundays. Getting to bed early on Saturday night and preparing breakfast and church clothes the night before can help, too.

Why make such a big deal about church? Because it benefits the kids as well as the adults to connect to God. Church gives us the opportunity to reflect on our blessings, which helps us to be more grateful. At church, we increase our social connections, learn to forgive, and find deeper meaning in our lives.

The next time you don't feel like going to church and think it's way too stressful to get everyone ready and out the door, remind yourself that is why you need to go to church. Church can help us deal with stress, which every family member needs.

Closing Thoughts from Steve

Perhaps you have observed a consistent theme in my comments in this book so far. It is a theme of self-evaluation, and it applies to having fun. First, if you are thinking of blending your family with another family and you are not a fun person, then ask yourself why you are doing this. Kids need to have parents who are fun. If you see your spouse's kids as a burden you must take on so you can be married, then you will be the burden on everyone. It is not right or fair to move into a home with kids, or to let them move into yours, if you are not free to have fun and enjoy them in the process.

My second consideration for you is not about you, but the one you are about to marry. Don't ruin the lives of your children by marrying someone who does not like them or does not know how to have fun with them. It would be better to be single than to bring problems onto yourself by being so desperate that you marry someone you know will never enjoy parenting your children. Be one of those courageous people who is strong enough to back out of the marriage before it starts. You will not regret it, and the sacrifice will be a blessing to you and your children.

When I started to get to know my stepsons Carter and James, I felt there was plenty of potential for fun—and I was the one who could create it. Madeline and I knew how to have fun, and she wanted brothers. We went to beaches, lakes, boats, cruises, trips, and threw and caught thousands of balls. We hiked, climbed, skied, sledded, built ice forts, and shot off real rockets and fireworks that sometimes exploded a bit too close to us. When I was speaking or taking New Life supporters on a trip, I would take one of the kids with me. Madeline went to Japan and Korea with me. Carter and I had a dinner in front of the Sydney Australia opera house. James and I rode camels in Petra, Jordan, where *Indiana Jones* was filmed. We always found a way to have fun.

Key Points to Remember

- Make fun an intentional activity.
- Fun, chores, routines, and traditions combined can create bonds in families.
- Each individual relationship in your home is important, so find ways to connect.
- Incorporate indoor and outdoor fun with your family.

CONCLUSION

A Challenge to Take Action

In this book we have looked at many ways to understand and love your bonus children. We have learned to accept realities of being a stepfamily as well as how to implement interpersonal skills to have a more successful one. We've gained knowledge about how to understand our children's personalities and how to help them manage stress, have fun, and increase their happiness. We've embraced the idea that we can not only survive but thrive as a stepfamily by using healthy communication and replacing our negative self-talk with the voice of truth.

There is a lot of information in this book. Try not to get overwhelmed. Keep building into the lives of your bonus children, even if they don't respond. Give it time. It will not happen overnight. Be patient with yourself as well as them.

Finishing this book is really a beginning, not an ending. Before you close the cover, I'd like to ask you to do one last thing: accept a challenge to take action. In order to see changes in your stepfamily, it is necessary to implement these ideas. Have faith that God will help you and bring to your mind the things that you have read in this book. Actions must flow from faith. Faith can change situations, save you from divorce, and help stepchildren. We have to be willing to step out of our comfort zones, take chances, and try new things, like the ideas in this book, even when we may initially find them difficult, awkward, or uncomfortable.

In the first chapter, I suggested six steps to ensure success in your stepfamily. Here they are again:

1. Recognize the areas in which your stepfamily needs to change.
2. Be purposeful in identifying the actions you need to take.
3. Follow through on your commitment to act.
4. Strive for small changes, not perfection.
5. Be patient with the process. Take living as a stepfamily one day at a time.
6. Seek God's help daily, as well as the support of others.

Only you and God know what new actions He is calling you to take. But I bet as you read these words, you already know in your heart what they are. Trust God with the outcomes as you try the new ideas and skills from this book. Pray to Him for guidance and direction.

Closing Thoughts from Steve

There are many choices that have an upside and a downside, but there are only two that have no downside: the choice to follow Jesus, and the choice to develop character. People of faith can get instruction from God, and people with character do what needs to be done when it needs to be done, no matter the consequences. No one has all of the character they need or all of the character possible because we are all human—but we can always develop more. Counseling, time alone with God, and a good Bible study help us grow in character. Do whatever it takes to become the person of character God calls you to be. That is the greatest contribution you can make to your bonus child.

A Stepparent's Prayer

Heavenly God,

I believe it is Your will that my stepfamily live in harmony and peace. I ask You to fill my mind with the knowledge I have read and to put that wisdom into action to better my marriage and love my bonus children. When I get discouraged, help me remember these Bible verses: For without Him, we can do nothing (John 15:5); and with Him, we can do anything (Philippians 4:13). God, I thank You that when the odds are against me, You are for me. I know You are with me and trust that You will be working behind the scenes for my family's good.

Amen

Notes

Chapter 1: The Bad, the Ugly, and the Good News about Bonus Families

1. Jamie M. Lewis and Rose M. Kreider, "Remarriage in the United States," American Community Survey Reports, U.S. Census Bureau, March 2015, https://www.census.gov/content/dam/Census/library/publications/2015/acs/acs-30.pdf.

2. Ron Deal, "Marriage, Family, & Stepfamily Statistics," updated 2021, https://smartstepfamilies.com/smart-help/marriage-family-stepfamily-statistics.

3. "A Portrait of Stepfamilies," Pew Research Center, January 13, 2011, http://pewsocialtrends.org/2011/01/13/a-portrait-of

-stepfamilies/. See also "The American Family Today," Pew Research Center, December 17, 2015, http://www.pewsocialtrends.org/2015/12/17/1-the-american-family-today.

4. Marla S. Miller, "The High Cost of Divorce," Miller Boileau Family Law Group, https://www.millerboileau.com/the-high-cost-of-divorce/.

5. "A Portrait of Stepfamilies"; See also "The American Family Today."

6. StepFamily Foundation of Alberta, "Stepfamily Facts," http://stepfamily.ca/stepfamily_facts.htm.

7. *Merriam-Webster Dictionary*, s.v. "fortitide, *n.*," https://www.merriam-webster.com/dictionary/fortitude.

8. Steve Arterburn, "Adversity Builds Character," *New Life Daily Devotional* email, January 18, 2021, https://mailchi.mp/192697adf6af/whats-wrong-with-grownups-5099308?e=d8c3750898.

9. T. D. Afifi, "Communication in Stepfamilies," in *The International Handbook of Stepfamilies: Policy and Practice in Legal, Research, and Clinical Environments*, ed. Jan

Pryor (Hoboken, NJ: Wiley & Sons, 2008), 299–322, https://doi.org/10.1002/9781118269923.

10. P. R. Amato, "The Implications of Research Findings on Children in Stepfamilies," in *Stepfamilies: Who Benefits? Who Does Not?*, eds. Alan Booth and Judy Dunn (Hillside, NJ: Lawrence Erlbaum, 2007), 81–88; Afifi, "Communication in Stepfamilies."; D. O. Braithwaite, C. M. McBride, and P. Schrodt, "'Parent Teams' and the Everyday Interactions of Co-parenting in Stepfamilies," *Communication Reports* 16, no. 2 (June 2003): 93–111; T. D. Afifi, "Stepfamily Communication Strengths: Understand the Ties That Bind," *Human Communication Research* 29, no. 1 (2003): 41–80; Patricia L. Papernow, "'Blended Family' Relationships: Helping People Who Live in Stepfamilies," *Family Therapy Magazine*, 2006, 34–42.

Chapter 2: Stepfamily Truths

1. Casting Crowns, "The Voice of Truth," track 3 on *Casting Crowns*, Beach Street Records, 2003.

Chapter 3: Accepting the Realities of Being a Stepfamily

1. Jeannette Lofas, "The Dynamics of Stepfamilies," *The Stepfamily Foundation*, February 5, 2014, https:\\www.stepfamily.org/blog/the-dynamics-of-stepfamilies.

2. Todd M. Jensen et al., "Stepfamily Relationship Quality and Children's Internalizing and Externalizing Problems," *Family Process* 57, no. 2 (2017): 477–95, https://doi.org/10.1111/famp.12284; Valarie King, "Stepfamily Formation: Implications for Adolescent Ties to Mothers, Nonresident Fathers, and Stepfathers," *Journal of Marriage and Family* 71, no. 4 (October 23, 2009): 954–68, https://doi.org/10.1111/j.1741-3737.2009.00646.x.

3. Anita Delongis and Melady Preece, "Emotional and Relational Consequences of Coping in Stepfamilies," *Marriage and Family Review* 34, no. 1–2 (January 2002): 118, https://doi.org/10.1300/J002v34n01_06.

Chapter 4: The Successful Stepfamily Marriage

1. Jamie M. Lewis and Rose M. Kreider, "Remarriage in the United States," American Community Survey Reports, U.S. Census Bureau, March 2015, https://www.census.gov/content/dam/Census/library/publications/2015/acs/acs-30.pdf.

2. C. Garneau, B. Higginbotham, and F. Adler-Baeder, "Remarriage Beliefs as Predictors of Marital Quality and Positive Interaction in Stepcouples," *Family Process* 54, no. 4 (2015): 730–45, https://doi.org/10.1111/famp.12153.

3. John Gottman and Nan Silver, *The Seven Principles for Making Marriage Work* (New York: Harmony, 2015).

4. Jeremy B. Yorgason et al., "Marital Benefits of Daily Individual and Conjoint Exercise among Older Couples," *Family Relations: Interdisciplinary Journal of Applied Family Science* 67, no. 2 (February 6, 2018): 227–39, https://doi.org/10.1111/fare.12307.

5. Gottman and Silver, *The Seven Principles for Making Marriage Work*.

6. Ibid.

Chapter 5: Helping Children Manage Stress in the Blended Family

1. Anita DeLongis and Ellen Stephenson, "A 20-Year Prospective Study of Marital Separation and Divorce in Stepfamilies: Appraisals of Family Stress as Predictors," *Journal of Social and Personal Relationships* 36, no. 6 (June 2019): 1600–18, https://doi.org/10.1177/0265407518768445.

2. Constance Ahrons, "Family Ties after Divorce: Long-Term Implications for Children," *Family Process* 46, no. 1 (February 2007): 53–65, https://doi.org/10.1111/j.1545-5300.2006.00191.x.

3. W. H. Jeynes, "The Impact of Parental Remarriage on Children: A Meta-Analysis," *Marriage & Family Review* 40, no. 4, (September 2008): 75–98, https://doi.org/10.1300/J002v40n04_05.

4. Jennifer Newcomb Marine and Jenna Korf, *Skirts At War: Beyond Divorced Mom/Stepmom Conflict* (CreateSpace, 2013).

5. Jeynes, "The Impact of Parental Remarriage on Children."

6. C. Cartwright, "Resident Parent–Child Relationships in Stepfamilies," in *The International Handbook of Stepfamilies: Policy and Practice in Legal, Research, and Clinical Environments*, ed. Jan Pryor (Hoboken, NJ: Wiley & Sons, 2008), 208–30, https://doi.org/ 10.1002/9781118269923.

Chapter 6: Conquering Difficulties

1. Lynn White and Joan G. Gilbreth, "When Children Have Two Fathers: Effects of Relationships with Stepfathers and Noncustodial Fathers on Adolescent Outcomes," *Journal of Marriage and Family* 63, no. 1 (2001): 155–67, https://doi.org/10.1111/j.1741-3737.2001.00155.x.

2. Katherine H. Shelton, Sasha L. Walters, and Gordon T. Harold, "Children's Appraisals of Relationships in Stepfamilies and First Families: Comparative Links with

Externalizing and Internalizing Behaviors," *The International Handbook of Stepfamilies: Policy and Practice in Legal, Research, and Clinical Environments,* ed. Jan Pryor (Hoboken, NJ: Wiley & Sons, 2008), 250–76, https://doi.org/10.1002/9781118269923.

3. Christy M. Buchanan and Kelly L. Heiges, "When Conflict Continues after the Marriage Ends: Effects of Postdivorce Conflict on Children," in *Interparental Conflict and Child Development: Theory, Research, and Application,* eds. J. H. Grych and F. D. Fincham (Cambridge: Cambridge University Press, 2001), 337–62, https://doi.org/10.1017/CBO9780511527838.015.

4. Gregory M. Fosco and John H. Grych, "Emotional, Cognitive, and Family Systems Mediators of Children's Adjustment to Interparental Conflict," *Journal of Family Psychology* 22, no. 6 (2008): 843–54, https://doi.org/10.1037/a0013809.

5. Mona El-Sheikh et al., "Sleep Disruptions and Emotional Insecurity Are Pathways of Risk for Children," *Journal of Child Psychology and Psychiatry* 48, no. 1 (2007): 88–96, https://doi.org/10.1111/j.1469-7610.2006.01604.x.

6. Paul R. Amato and Tamara D. Afifi, "Feeling Caught between Parents: Adult Children's Relations with Parents and Subjective Well-Being," *Journal of Marriage and Family* 68, no. 1 (February 2006): 222–35, https://doi.org/10.1111 /j.1741-3737.2006.00243.x.

7. Constance Ahrons, *We're Still Family: What Grown Children Have to Say About Their Parents' Divorce* (New York: HarperCollins, 2004).

8. Jan Pryor, "Resilience in Stepfamilies," (prepared for Centre for Social Research and Evaluation, funded by the Ministry of Social Development, Wellington, New Zealand, July 2004).

9. Daniel G. Amen, *Change Your Brain, Change Your Life* (New York: Three Rivers Press, 1998).

Chapter 7: Healthy Communication in Stepfamilies

1. T. D. Afifi, "Communication in Stepfamilies," in *The International Handbook of Stepfamilies: Policy and Practice in Legal, Research, and Clinical Environments*, ed. Jan Pryor (Hoboken, NJ: Wiley & Sons, 2008), 299–322, https:// doi.org/10.1002/9781118269923.

2. Patricia Papernow, "Clinical Guidelines for Working with Stepfamilies: What Family, Couple, Individual, and Child

Therapists Need to Know," *Family Process* 57, no. 1 (October 2017): 25–51, https://doi.org/10.1111/famp.12321.

3. L. Ganong, M. Coleman, and T. Jamison, "Patterns of Stepchild-Stepparent Relationship Development," *Journal of Marriage and Family* 73, no. 2 (April 2011): 396–413, https://doi.org/10.1111/j.1741-3737.2010.00814.x.

4. S. M. Stanley, S. L. Blumberg, and H. J. Markman, "Helping Couples Fight for Their Marriages," in *Preventive Approaches in Couples Therapy*, eds. Rony Berger and Mo Therese Hannah (New York: Brunner/Mazel, 1999), 279–303.

5. John M. Gottman, *The Science of Trust: Emotional Attunement for Couples* (New York: Norton, 2011).

6. Gottman, *The Science of Trust*.

7. Patricia L. Papernow, "Post-Divorce Parenting: A Baker's Dozen of Suggestions for Protecting Children," *Family Mediation Quarterly* 1, no. 2 (Fall 2002): 6–10, https://mcfm.org/sites/default/files/FMQ/fall02.pdf.

8. Lysa TerKeurst (@LysaTerKeurst), "Oh friend…let's remember that words are never just syllables and nouns…," Twitter, April 10, 2021, 10:00 a.m., https://mobile.twitter.com/LysaTerKeurst/status/1380883290643652608.

9. Papernow, "Clinical Guidelines for Working with Stepfamilies."

Chapter 8: Interpersonal Skills for Stepfamilies

1. P. R. Amato, "The Implications of Research Findings on Children in Stepfamilies," in *Stepfamilies: Who Benefits? Who Does Not?*, eds. Alan Booth and Judy Dunn (Hillside, NJ: Lawrence Erlbaum, 2007), 81–88; T. D. Afifi, "Communication in Stepfamilies," in *The International Handbook of Stepfamilies,* ed. Jan Pryor (Hoboken, NJ: Wiley & Sons, 2008), 299–322; D. O. Braithwaite, C. M. McBride, and P. Schrodt, "'Parent Teams' and the Everyday Interactions of Co-parenting in Stepfamilies," *Communication Reports* 16, no. 2 (June 2003): 93–111; T. D. Afifi, "Stepfamily Communication Strengths: Understand the Ties That Bind," *Human Communication Research* 29, no. 1 (2003): 41–80; Patricia L. Papernow, "'Blended Family' Relationships: Helping People Who Live in Stepfamilies," *Family Therapy Magazine*, 2006, 34–42.

2. Afifi, "Communication in Stepfamilies."

3. John Gottman and Joan DeClaire, *Raising an Emotionally Intelligent Child* (New York: Simon & Schuster, 1996).

Chapter 9: Understanding Your Bonus Child's Personality

1. Florence Littauer, *Personality Plus* (Grand Rapids, MI: Revell, 1992).

2. Gary Chapman, *The 5 Love Languages of Children: The Secret to Loving Children Effectively* (Chicago: Northfield Publishing, 2016).

3. Milan and Kay Yerkovich, *How We Love* (New York: WaterBrook, 2017).

4. Chapman, *The 5 Love Languages of Children.*

5. Gary Chapman and Ron L. Deal, *Building Love Together in Blended Families: The 5 Love Languages and Becoming Stepfamily Smart* (Chicago: Northfield Publishing, 2020).

6. Milan and Kay Yerkovich, *How We Love Our Kids: The Five Love Styles of Parenting* (New York: WaterBrook, 2011).

Chapter 10: Increasing Happiness in Stepchildren

1. Barbara L. Fredrickson, *Positivity: Groundbreaking Research Reveals How to Embrace the Hidden Strength of Positive Emotions, Overcome Negativity, and Thrive* (New York: Crown Publishing, 2009).

2. Andrew N. Meltzoff, "Imitation and Other Minds: The 'Like Me' Hypothesis," in *Perspectives on Imitation: From Cognitive Neuroscience to Social Science*, vol. 2 (Cambridge, MA: MIT Press, 2005), 55–77.

3. Bruce Feiler, *The Secrets of Happy Families: Improve Your Mornings, Tell Your Family History, Fight Smarter, Go Out and Play, and Much More* (New York: William Morrow Paperbacks, 2013).

4. *Macmillan Dictionary*, s.v. "coddle, *v.*," https://www .macmillandictionary.com/us/dictionary/american/coddle.

5. Bonnie Harris, *When Your Kids Push Your Buttons: And What You Can Do About It* (New York: Warner Books, Inc., 2003).

6. Julie Lythcott-Haims, *How to Raise an Adult* (New York: St. Martin's Press, 2015).

7. Stuart Brown and Christopher Vaughan, *Play: How It Shapes the Brain, Opens the Imagination, and Invigorates the Soul* (New York: Avery, 2009).

8. Bob Murray and Alicia Fortinberry, *Raising an Optimistic Child: A Proven Plan for Depression-Proofing Young*

Children—For Life (New York: McGraw-Hill Education, 2006).

9. Christine Carter, *Raising Happiness: 10 Simple Steps for More Joyful Kids and Happier Parents* (New York: Ballantine Books, 2011).

10. Jeffrey J. Froh, William J. Sefick, and Robert A. Emmonds, "Counting Blessings in Early Adolescents: An Experimental Study of Gratitude and Subjective Well-Being," *Journal of School Psychology* 46, no. 2 (2008): 213–33, https://doi.org/10.1016/j.jsp.2007.03.005.

11. Carter, *Raising Happiness.*

12. John Gottman and Joan DeClaire, *Raising an Emotionally Intelligent Child* (New York: Simon & Schuster, 1996).